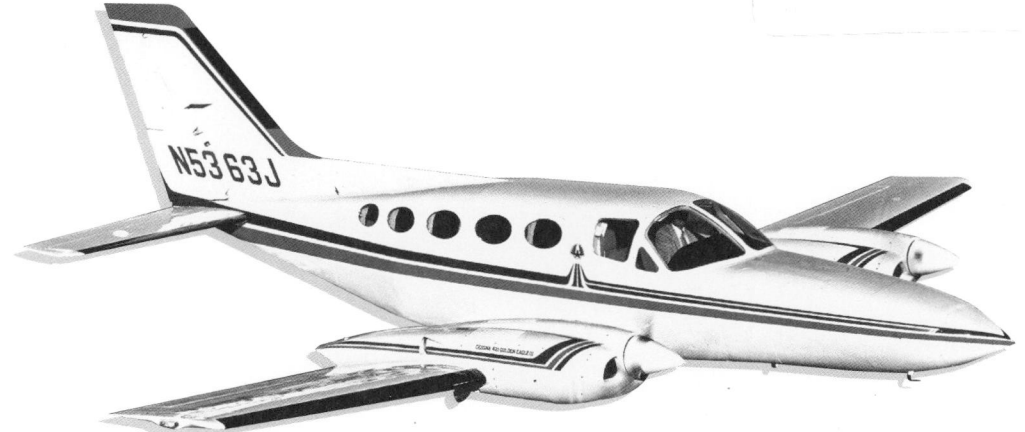

Ron Smith

TWIN
CESSNA

The Cessna
300 and 400 Series
of Light Twins

Schiffer Publishing Ltd

4880 Lower Valley Road • Atglen, PA 19310

Designed by Molly Shields
Type set in Berthold Akzidenz Grotesk BE/Caxton Bk BT

ISBN: 978-0-7643-5226-3
Printed in China

Published by Schiffer Publishing, Ltd.
4880 Lower Valley Road
Atglen, PA 19310
Phone: (610) 593-1777; Fax: (610) 593-2002
E-mail: Info@schifferbooks.com

For our complete selection of fine books on this and related subjects, please visit our website at www.schifferbooks.com. You may also write for a free catalog.

This book may be purchased from the publisher. Please try your bookstore first.

We are always looking for people to write books on new and related subjects. If you have an idea for a book, please contact us at proposals@schifferbooks.com.

Schiffer Publishing's titles are available at special discounts for bulk purchases for sales promotions or premiums. Special editions, including personalized covers, corporate imprints, and excerpts can be created in large quantities for special needs. For more information, contact the publisher.

Contents

Introduction and Acknowledgments

Up until the early 1950s, there was only one type of twin Cessna: the wartime Cessna T-50 Crane or UC-78 Bobcat navigation trainer. This rounded design, with its rumbling 245 hp Jacobs engines, carried five occupants at speeds up to around 190 mph. It was affectionately known as the "Bamboo Bomber" due to its use of wood and fabric wing construction and its fabric-covered steel tube fuselage, minimizing the use of more strategic materials. The Bobcat weighed-in at 5,000 lb. and had a quoted maximum range of 750 miles.

In 1953, however, Cessna introduced the Cessna 310, a fast, clean, almost fighter-like, five seat, retractable undercarriage twin-engine aircraft for private and executive use.

A colorful Cessna Bobcat N58542 photographed in 1990 at Vancouver, Washington. *Jim Smith*

Cessna UC-78B Bobcat 42-71626 exhibited at the USAF Museum, Dayton, Ohio. *US Air Force photograph*

This attractive and successful aircraft remained in production until 1981, and established twin-engine designs as an important product line at Cessna. By comparison with the Bobcat, the first production Cessna 310 aircraft carried the same number of occupants, on much the same power at 4,600 lb. gross weight. The cruise speed at 75% power was up to 210 mph and the range, cruising at 60% power, was some 810 miles.

These figures are somewhat comparable, but the two aircraft could not have been more different in appearance and style. The Bobcat was in many ways the end of the line, whereas the Cessna 310 represented the start of a new breed of high performance light aircraft. This included both the 300-series of twin-engine aircraft and the larger Cessna 400 series of "cabin-class" executive, air taxi and commuter types. These are the subjects of this work.

The prototype Cessna 310 N41699 seen outside the Cessna factory in 1953. *Cessna Aircraft Company*

The Cessna 336
Skymaster and 337
Super Skymaster fall
outside the scope of
this work. N2657S is
a Cessna 337C
photographed on the
approach to Hicks
Field, Texas. *Author*

Cessna T303
Crusader G-PUSI
photographed at its
home base of
Henstridge in Dorset
in June 2010. *Author*

This volume restricts discussion to the conventionally configured twins in the Cessna -300 and -400 series of aircraft. It does not include the less conventional "push-me, pull-you" Cessna 336 and 337 Skymaster and Super Skymaster.

For convenience, the book is split into two main sections: the Cessna 300-series, and the Cessna 400-series. The 300-series includes the closely related Cessna 310 and 320; the Cessna 340 and its unpressurized version, the Cessna 335; and finally the Cessna T303 Crusader.

The 400-series ranges from the Cessna 411 first flown in 1962 and produced until 1968, through a family of similar aircraft (C401 and C402, C404, C414, and C421), followed by the turbo-prop C425 and C441, produced until 1987. Finally, there is the French-built F406 Caravan II, which entered production in 1985. The Cessna 400 series spanned applications from private, air taxi, and executive use, through to operation as a third-level feederliner.

Each section also includes a discussion of the experience of owning and flying selected examples of the family, for which particular thanks are due to Justin Cox (Cessna 310), Roche Bentley (Cessna T303), and Patrick Caruth (Cessna 404).

• • •

Many of the photographs are from the author's own collection. Photographs have also been most generously supplied by the Cessna Aircraft Company and by the author's twin brother, Jim Smith. Particular thanks are due to Rick

Cessna 441 Conquest II VH-VEM at Canberra, ACT, Australia, in December 2004. *Jim Smith*

Reitmeyer at Cessna Aircraft for providing some specific images to complete the picture.

Acknowledgement must also be made of the images kindly supplied by the following: Chris Arrington, Gary Chambers; Barry Collman; Justin Cox, Patrick Caruth, Peter Davison, Clive and Glenn Denney (www.merlinsovermalta.com); Derek Heley; Jason LeMay of the Kentucky National Guard e-museum; Debbie O'Sullivan of the British Meteorological Office; Joe Renda, Bay Air Aircraft Sales; Mike Rowland of the Museum of Aviation, Warner Robbins AFB; Jerry Temple of Jerry Temple Aviation Inc.; the USAF Museum; and Ad Vercruijsse (http://www.aviator.nl).

Where aircraft production numbers are quoted, these have generally been taken from the serial number listings contained in the relevant FAA Type Certificate Data Sheets. Where possible, these have also been crosschecked with Rod Simpson's excellent *Airlife's General Aviation* (Airlife 1991). Descriptions of the differences between models have been typically been derived from that reference; from editions of *Janes All The World's Aircraft,* and (for the Cessna 310 and 320) from the relevant section of William D Thompson's *Cessna Wings for the World.*

Part A: Cessna 300 Series

The production of the various aircraft within the Cessna 300 series overlapped in time and the various types are presented in sequence by each type's first flight date. The overall timelines for the production of the Cessna 300 series are shown in the diagram.

Production of the Cessna 310 ran through a range of models from 1953 to 1981. In parallel, the closely related Cessna 320 was produced from 1962 until 1968. A new design, the Cessna 340 was introduced in 1970 and produced until 1985. A sub-variant, the Cessna 335, was only produced as a 1980 model. Finally, a further new model, the Cessna T303 was introduced, its production running from 1979 until 1985. This is therefore the sequence in which these models are discussed below.

TIMELINES FOR MODELS
within the Cessna 300 series

C320
1962-68

1950

1960

C310
1953

Three Ten i

N800IM

T303
1979-85

C335
1980

C340
1970-85

C310R
1981

1970

1980

Cessna 310

This first section reviews the background to the introduction of the Cessna 310, together with a summary of its main competitors. This is followed by a top-level description of the Cessna 310's design features.

The individual models in the range are then described and illustrated in sequence, with an indication of the main changes and sub-variants introduced during their production. After-market modifications are also discussed, where relevant.

Overview, Origins, and Competition

Although a number of references describe the Cessna 310 as the first modern light twin, a number of other designs in this category were already in production when the prototype Cessna 310 N41699 flew for the first time on January 3, 1953. Among these were the Aero Commander 520, the Beechcraft Twin Bonanza, and the Piper Apache.

The Aero Commander family originated with the Aero Commander L.3085, which first flew in April 1948. This high wing design entered production as the Aero Commander 520, receiving its FAA type certificate in January 1952. The 520 was powered by two 290 hp Lycoming GO-435-C engines. The Aero Commander family was successfully developed into a wide range of piston and turboprop-powered models, continuing in production with Rockwell and then Gulfstream American until 1985.

William D Thomson in *Cessna Wings for the World* comments that the Aero Commander designer Ted Smith sounded out Cessna as to their interest in producing the design. Cessna had their own plans, however, and considered that the Aero Commander would be expensive to manufacture and was somewhat lacking in engine out performance.

The six-seat Beechcraft 50 Twin Bonanza betrays its origins in its name, as a twin engine development of Beechcraft's popular and high performance Bonanza. The first prototype was flown in November 1949, entering production in 1952 for both civilian and military users (the latter under the designations L-23A, B, and D). Power was initially provided by a pair of 290 hp Lycoming GO-435-C engines. The Twin Bonanza remained in production until 1963; the last model produced being the J50, by which time the power was provided by two 340 hp Lycoming GSIO-480-A1A6 engines. The maximum take-off weight had also increased from 5,500 lb. to 7,300 lb. during the type's production run. In total, 974 Twin Bonanza aircraft of all models were produced.

The Aero Commander was already in production when the Cessna 310 was first flown. This as an Aero Commander 560 photographed at Terrell, Texas. *Author*

The Beechcraft Twin Bonanza first flew in 1962. This is an RU-8D Seminole 58-3086 (N130AZ) in US Army color scheme. *Author*

The final version of the Twin Bonanza was the J50; this is VH-BRH, a 1962 example, photographed at Avalon, VIC, Australia, in March 2009. *Jim Smith*

Another competitor for the Cessna 310 was the Piper Apache. This photograph shows a 1961 PA-23-160 Apache G-ARJU at the hilltop airfield of Compton Abbas, Dorset, UK. *Author*

The final competitor, whose development and production timescales made it a close contemporary of the Cessna 310, was the Piper PA-23 Apache (and its later development, the Aztec). The Apache was a slightly portly low wing design that owed its origins to the Twin Stinson, for which Piper had acquired the production rights in 1948.

Piper modified this design to become the PA-23 Apache, whose prototype flew in March 1952. Type certification followed in 1954, after which the Apache entered production.

The Apache was initially powered by two 150 hp Lycoming O-320 engines, this being successively increased to 160 hp and then 235 hp on each side. A further increase in engine power to 250 hp, together with a longer fuselage and swept fin, resulted in a name change to the Aztec. During the type's development and production, maximum weight was increased from 3,500 to 4,800 lb. These models were very successful, with 2,165 Apache, and 4,811 Aztecs being manufactured between 1954 and 1981.

The Piper Apache is a close contemporary of the Cessna 310, having first flown in 1952. N1393P is a 1956 example and is fitted with a non-standard dorsal fin. *Author*

A fine air to air photograph of the 1953 prototype of the
Cessna 310 N41699. *Cessna Aircraft*

The ground breaking Cessna 310 appeared in 1953. The prototypes were initially powered by a pair of 225 hp engines, these being replaced by a pair of 240 hp Continental O-470 B in the 1954 production model. During initial development the decision was also taken to increase the seating capacity from four to five seats, this also requiring an increase in tailplane area to provide an increased aft center of gravity limit.

Characteristics

The Cessna 310 stood out as soon as it appeared with its clean lines, tightly cowled and streamlined engine installation and wing tip fuel tanks that allowed a thinner wing to be used. The fin was unswept and seats were provided for five

Cessna 310 N5302A (c/n 35502) photographed at North Las Vegas Airport, Nevada. The over-wing exhaust augmentor tube outlets are clearly shown. *Author*

VH-REK is a Cessna 310B, photographed at Goulburn, NSW, Australia in April 2013. *Author*

occupants—two in the cockpit and three sat abreast in the cabin. Access to the cockpit and cabin was provided by a single door on the starboard side, with a fixed foot step conveniently located at the rear of wing root. A grab handle of the upper fuselage side to the rear further aids entry.

The engine installation also featured an exhaust system terminating over the wing in two exhaust thrust augmentor tubes exiting some way ahead of the wing trailing edge. These entrained air from the cowling, providing increased cooling airflow at high power levels.

With its clean, fighter-like design, the Cessna 310 was lighter and lower powered than either the Aero Commander or the Twin Bonanza while offering similar capacity and performance. It also offered significantly higher performance than the Apache. The Cessna 310 remained in production until the end of 1981, the final model being the shark-like 310R with its long pointed nose, swept fin, and smaller ventral fin.

Cessna 310 Variants

Cessna 310 to 310C and U-3A (Straight Tail, Early Tip Tank Shape)

The early production variants of the Cessna 310, the Cessna 310, 310A (U-3A), 310B, and 310C are visually very similar to each other. They share the unswept fin profile and feature the initial shape of tip tank (known by some as the "tuna tank').

The Cessna 310 received its FAA type approval on March 22, 1954, and was fitted with two Continental O-470-B, or -M engines of 240 hp. Its dimensions were: wingspan was 35.77 ft; fuselage length 26.9 ft; and the overall height 10.5 ft. The maximum permissible take-off weight was 4,600 lb. The fuel capacity was 102 US gallons, split between the two tip tanks. There were no integral wing tanks or other auxiliary fuel. The allowable baggage capacity was 200 lb.

The 1957 Cessna 310 N924RC at North Las Vegas Airport, Nevada. *Author*

The wing was fitted with split flaps, these being lowered to 45 degrees for landing. Both the flaps and the inward retracting undercarriage are electrically operated. Quoted performance includes a maximum speed of 223 mph at sea level; a 70% power cruise speed at 10,000 ft. of 205 mph; sea level climb rate of 1,700 ft/min and single engine service ceiling of 7,500 ft. Single engine climb rate is quoted as 380 ft./min.

Cessna 310 G-APNJ is preserved at the Newark Air Museum, Newark, UK. *Author*

The magazine *Flight International* reported on a flight test in September 1955, describing the type as "satisfying and exhilarating to fly." The article commented, however, on the relatively low maneuvering speed of 159 mph, compared with its cruising speed in excess of 200 mph, restricting handling to "gentle maneuvers" only in the cruise.

The type featured exceptional roll control but was regarded by *Flight* as having only neutral pitch stability. This subsequently led to the use of springs and weights in the elevator circuit of the later models to provide adequate longitudinal stability at higher weights and with extended aft center of gravity limits. In all, 547 Cessna 310s were built.

The next variant was the Cessna 310A. This type was produced for US Air Force service as a communications aircraft, entering service as the L-27A and subsequently being re-designated the U-3A.

This variant received its type approval on April 9, 1957. It was in most respects identical to the Cessna 310; the maximum take-off weight was increased to 4,830 lb., but the maximum landing weight remained at 4,600 lb. The type was fitted with Continental O-470-M engines and was also fitted with military-specific equipment and received a different elevator downspring.

Cessna U-3A Blue Canoe 58-2124, exhibited at the USAF Museum, Dayton, Ohio. *US Air Force photograph*

A damaged U-3A 58-2160 photographed at Fort Worth, Texas, in December 1989. This aircraft was later restored to the civil register as N5972. *Jim Smith*

Cessna 310B OO-SED/N611CE photographed at Cranfield, Bedfordshire, UK in 1986, wearing the color scheme of the Sabena Airlines Training Academy. *Author*

N1705H is a 1959 Cessna 310C. *Peter Davison*

A total of 160 U-3A/Cessna 310As were built and a number of aircraft transferred to the civilian register after leaving military service. The USAF used an attractive navy blue and white color scheme for the type and it became popularly known as the "Blue Canoe," although the reasons for this are not clear.

The next version for the civil market was the Cessna 310B, which received its type approval on May 23, 1957. This model was essentially identical to the Cessna 310, other than permitting a maximum take-off weight of 4,700 lb; the maximum landing weight remained at 4,600 lb. As with the Cessna 310A, Continental O-470-M engines were fitted. A total of 224 Cessna 310Bs were built

The 1959 production model was the Cessna 310C, which was the last version with an unswept tail fin. The 310C received its type approval on October 22, 1958. The main visual difference from the earlier models was the rearward extension of the over-wing nacelle to the trailing edge, the exhaust exiting through a rectangular aperture.

Power for the Cessna 310C was provided by two 260 hp IO-470-D engines. The maximum take-off weight was increased to 4,830 lb., the maximum landing weight remaining at 4,600 lb. A total of 260 Cessna 310Cs were built.

A gleaming, polished Cessna 310C VH-DBA at Goulburn, NSW, Australia, in April 2013.
Author

Additional Cessna 310 to Cessna 310C Images

Cessna 310 F-BKBS with a non-standard rear cabin window, similar to that used on the Riley Rocket. This aircraft, which was photographed at Toussus-Le-Noble, France, was previously registered as G-ARGP (without the extra window). *Author*

N8063X is a civilianized Cessna U-3A Blue Canoe, previously 57-5910. It was photographed at North Las Vegas Airport, Nevada. *Author*

The clean lines of Cessna 310B in the Australian sunshine at Goulburn NSW in April 2013. *Author*

An attractive photograph of Cessna U-3A Blue Canoe 58-2124, exhibited at the USAF Museum, Dayton, Ohio. *US Air Force photograph*

An immaculate Cessna 310C N6710T, photographed at Oshkosh, Wisconsin. *Author*

G-AVZS is a 1958 Cessna 310B photographed at Fairoaks Airport, Surrey. *Author*

Cessna 310D to 310F, including U-3B (Swept Fin, Early Tip Tank Shape)

The next variant of the Cessna 310, the 1960 Cessna 310D, introduced a swept fin, bringing the styling into line with other contemporary Cessna models such as the Cessna 172, whose 1960 model Cessna 172A gained its "flight sweep" fin. The Cessna 310D retained the 260 hp IO-470-D engines fitted to the previous year's model. Type approval was gained on 8 July 1959 and a total of 268 of this variant were built. In other respects (take-off and landing weight; center of gravity range; baggage capacity; and fuel capacity) the 310D had the same specification as the 1959 Cessna 310C.

The Cessna 310E and Cessna 310F are visually identical. The C310E was another communications aircraft for the USAF, taken into service as the U-27B, later allocated the designation U-3B. Both this aircraft and the Cessna 310F had a third side window and (310F) a more pointed nose shape, these being externally distinguishing features from the previous model.

A total of thirty-six Cessna 310E (U-3B) is widely quoted as having been produced. The FAA Type Certificate Data

The Cessna 310E and F have an additional cabin window. Thirty-six examples of the 310E were built and delivered to the USAF for communications duties as the L-27B/U-3B. This example is displayed at the Museum of Aviation, Warner Robins AFB, Georgia. *Mike Rowland*

A swept fin was introduced with the 1960 Cessna 310D. This example, N6839T was photographed in August 1995, at Norwood Memorial Airport, Massachusetts. *Derek Heley*

Sheet lists thirty-seven applicable serial numbers. The U-3B was permitted increased take-off and landing weights, these being, respectively 4,990 and 4,750 lb. A restricted forward center of gravity limit applied at maximum take-off weight. This model received its type approval on September 21, 1959.

Aircraft that were returned to the civilian register after USAF service are also designated Cessna 310M.

The very similar Cessna 310F received its type approval on July 25, 1960, becoming the 1961 production model. Maximum weights for this civilian model were restored to the previous figures of 4,830 lb. for take-off and 4,600 lb. for landing. A total of 156 310Fs were built.

Cessna 310Es were given construction numbers in a sequence from 310M001, civilianized examples also being known as the Cessna 310M. N5077K was photographed at Oshkosh, Wisconsin, and was previously USAF 60-6062. *Author*

Additional U-3B Images

An immaculate U-3B/310M N5076A, in the Florida sunshine at Sun 'n Fun at Linder Regional Airport in March 2012. This aircraft was previously USAF 60-6063. *John Yates*

Kentucky National Guard U-3A 60-6072 taxies past the camera. *Gary Chambers*

Cessna 310F N6746X has found its last resting place at Sharjah International Airport in the UAE, where it was photographed in June 1999. *Peter Davison*

Cessna 310G to C310P: Swept Fin and Canted "Stabila-tip" Tip Tanks

The initial Cessna 310 model was produced without change of designation from 1954 until the C310A model appeared in 1957. Thereafter, each succeeding year was marked by evolution of the design, the model year being reflected in changes in the designation suffix letter. The preceding discussion has taken us to the 1962 Cessna 310F.

In 1963, there was a further significant change in external appearance with the introduction of a new pointed and upward canted wing tip tank on the Cessna 310G. In Cessna marketing terminology, this was the "stabila-tip." Yearly changes in model number continued encompassing the C310G, H, I, J, K, L, N, and P in sequence from 1963 until 1969.

The main differences between these models are summarized below, highlighting externally differentiating features and briefly covering other key changes in specification such as installed power and engine model, seating capacity, maximum weights, changes in maximum flap deflection, etc.

Cessna 310G

This was the first model to be fitted with the stabila-tip wing tip tanks. These had an identical capacity to the original tip tank and contributed to lateral stability by an increase in the dihedral effect. The 310G received its type approval on October 2, 1961, becoming the 1962 production model. The cabin area was increased and, although the standard layout provided five seats, an optional six-seat arrangement was also available. The engines remained unchanged, the type using the 260 hp Continental IO-470-D. Operating weights were increased to those of the U-3B, namely maximum take-off 4,990 lb., landing 4,750 lb. A total of 156 Cessna 310Gs were built.

The 1962 Cessna 310G introduced canted "stabila-tip" tip tanks. This is G-ASYV (later to become G-XITD) at Booker (Wycombe Air Park), Bucks. *Author*

Cessna 310H

This was the 1963 production model, receiving its type approval on July 19, 1962. The engines remained unchanged, the type using the 260 hp Continental IO-470-D. Maximum all up weight (take-off and landing) was increased to 5,100 lb. A total of 148 Cessna 310Hs were built (based on the Type Certificate Data Sheet data).

VH-WRG is a 1963 Cessna 310H (c/n 310H 0030, previously N1030Q), photographed in July 1970. *Peter Davison*

Cessna 310I

This was the first model to replace the over-wing exhaust system with twin exhausts underneath the engine cowling. The opportunity was taken to lengthen the engine nacelles rearward, beyond the wing trailing edge, to provide additional baggage stowage at the rear of the extended nacelle. This arrangement increased the baggage capacity to no less than 600 lb., made up of 200 lb. in the normal baggage compartment, 160 lb. on the cabin floor and 120 lb. in each nacelle baggage bay.

The 310I received its type approval on October 2, 1961, becoming the 1962 production model. The engines were updated to the Continental IO-470-U, maximum power remaining 260hp. The standard fuel capacity remained at 102 US gal. in the tip tanks, but Cessna could also supply auxiliary tankage, increasing total capacity to 133 US gal.

Operating weights were increased to a maximum of 5,100 lb. for both take-off and landing. Maximum landing flap deflection was reduced from 45 to 35 degrees. Cessna quoted a standard empty weight of 3,094 lb. for this model, although like all such manufacturer's empty weight data, this figure should be treated with some caution. Other performance data quoted by Cessna included: five or six seat capacity; maximum speed 238 mph; max cruise at 75% power at 6,500 ft. 223 mph; rate of climb 1,590 ft/min; and range on standard fuel at 6,500 ft. 780 miles. A total of 200 Cessna 310Is were built.

The 1964 Cessna 310I introduced underwing exhausts and extended nacelles containing baggage compartments. *Cessna Aircraft Company*

Cessna 310I G-MEBC photographed at Cranfield, Bedfordshire, UK. This aircraft was damaged beyond repair in a landing accident at Goodwood in March 1994. *Author*

Cessna 310J

The 310J received its type approval on September 3, 1964, becoming the 1965 production model. Changes from the previous year's model were minor, although there was another change in the bob weight in the elevator control system – the elevator control system was modified between many of the models. The engines and operating weights remained unchanged from those of the 310I. A total of 200 310Js were built.

G-ODLY is a Cessna 310J, photographed at Halfpenny Green. This aircraft was subsequently sold in the United States. *Author*

Cessna 310J G-ATCS photographed in a very appealing paint scheme at Biggin Hill, Kent, UK. *Jim Smith*

Cessna 310K

The Cessna 310K introduced long side windows on either side of the cabin, further enhancing the fighter-like appearance of the type. In typical Cessna marketing speak, these were known as "vista-view" windows. The 310K received its type approval on October 20, 1965, becoming the 1966 production model. The engine model was changed to the Continental IO-470-V or –VO, rated power remaining at 260 hp. Operating weights were increased to 5,200 lb. for both take-off and landing. A total of 245 Cessna 310Ks were built.

The 1966 Cessna 310K introduced long side windows, providing in Cessna's description a "vista-view." VH-CKB was photographed at Caloundra, QLD, Australia. *Author*

Cessna 310L

This model featured a single-piece, rather than two-piece windscreen. It also offered a substantial increase in the maximum fuel capacity from 102 US gal. to either 143 US gal. or 183 US gal. These figures are respectively achieved by fitting an auxiliary tank in each wing (adding 41 US gal. to the total) and then adding a 20 gal. transfer tank in each wing locker. The disadvantage of this is, perhaps, a rather complex system requiring careful fuel management.

The 310L received its type approval on September 20, 1966, becoming the 1967 production model. Flap and gear limiting speeds were increased to 160 mph, compared with 140 mph for the previous model. Other key parameters remained unchanged. A total of 207 Cessna 310Ls were built.

Cessna 310L G-BBBX on short finals to land at Southampton Airport, Hampshire, UK. *Author*

Cessna 310N

The 310N received its type approval on August 22, 1967, becoming the 1968 production model. Other than a revised instrument panel, there was little change from the previous model. Power was unchanged, this model using Continental IO-470-VO or IO-470-V engines. A total of 198 Cessna 310Ns were built.

Cessna 310P

The final model in this group is the Cessna 310P, which received its type approval on August 30, 1968, becoming the 1969 production model. This model introduced a small ventral fin to maintain directional stability. The undercarriage nose leg was also shortened. The Continental IO-470-VO was fitted as standard, but a turbo-charged version, the T310P, was also available, powered by two 285 hp Continental TSIO-520-B or –BB engines. This variant received its type approval on the same date as the 310P and is permitted maximum take-off and landing weights of 5,400 lb., 200 lb. more than the normally aspirated model. A total of 240 310Ps (of both types) were built.

Cessna 310Q and 310R: Production Models from 1970 to 1981 (Raised Rear Cabin Roof Line)

From 1970, Cessna abandoned the use of a letter suffix to indicate yearly upgrades to the Cessna 310. From this point onward, only two model designations were used until production ceased at the end of 1981. These two variants were the Cessna 310Q and the Cessna 310R (with their turbocharged sub-variants, the T310Q and the T310R).

This decision is reflected in the production quantities, with 1,160 310Q and 1,332 310R being manufactured (including both normally aspirated and turbocharged versions). This compares with annual production quantities of typically 200 aircraft for the earlier models. In fact, production of these two models, at a combined total of 2,492, represents a significant proportion of the total production of around 6,000 aircraft.

Cessna 310Q and T310Q

The 310Q and T310Q received their type approvals on August 20, 1969, and were produced from 1970 to 1974. Power was provided by the 260 hp IO-470-VO (310Q) or 285 hp TSIO-520-B or –BB (T310Q). The maximum take-off and landing weights were 5,300 lb. for the 310Q and 5,500 lb. (take-off) and 5,400 (landing) for the T310Q.

Cessna 310Q I-NEMM, photographed in the Varese area of northern Italy. This is 310Q-0101, a pre-1972 aircraft without the raised rear cabin and "omni-vision" window. *Author*

OE-FAX is an immaculate Cessna 310Q (c/n 310Q-0071) photographed in August 1971. *Peter Davison*

G-BAHW is a 1973 Cessna 310Q with raised rear window at Southampton Airport, Hampshire, UK. *Author*

The most significant change during the production run of the 310Q was that the rear cabin height was raised in 1972 (from aircraft 0401 onward), allowing a rear window to be introduced for the benefit of the rear seat passengers. In best marketing fashion, Cessna called this the "omni-vision" window. A larger ventral fin was introduced to maintain directional stability.

Cessna's approximate empty weight for the 1972 310Q was stated as 3,214 lb., compared with 3,094 lb. for the 1964 310I. A further auxiliary tank option was available, increasing the maximum capacity to no less than 203 US gallons. This was made up of tip tanks (100 US gal. usable), wing locker tanks (40 US gal. usable), and wing auxiliary tanks (63 US gal. usable). Fuel management was made somewhat complex by the fact that the wing locker tanks do not feed the engines directly; their contents must first be pumped across to the tip tanks. Also, the auxiliary tanks cannot be used with full tip tanks. This requires good planning to ensure that fuel is managed effectively as the flight proceeds and that the pilot maintains an accurate understanding of fuel levels at all times.

A new 15 degree flap limiting speed of 180 mph (160 kt) was also introduced for the 310Q and T310Q. As previously noted, *Flight* magazine had commented in 1955 on the relatively low maneuvering speed of the Cessna 310 compared with its high cruising speed. This remained the case with later models, including the 310Q, which could cruise at 221 mph, well beyond the maximum maneuver speed of 170 mph. A total of 1,160 310Q/T310Qs were built.

G-BARG is a 1973 E310Q (E variants have somewhat lower operating weights) on its landing approach. The nacelle lockers, "vista-view" and "omni-vision" windows are clearly visible. *Author*

Cessna 310Q N7561Q photographed at Shobdon, Herefordshire, UK. The inner exhaust has produced a large soot stain on the undercarriage leg. *Author*

Additional Cessna 310Q Images

I-DRAC is a Cessna T310Q, photographed in June 1971.
Peter Davison

Yugoslav Cessna 310Q (c/n 310Q-0041) photographed at Elstree, UK, in January 1986. This aircraft was subsequently registered as G-BMMC and G-XLKF before being sold in the United States.
Peter Davison

Cessna 310R and T310R

The final production model was the Cessna 310R (and its turbocharged variant the T310R). Both types received their type approval on 15 August 1974, being produced from 1975 to 1981. Power was provided by two 285 hp Continental IO-520-M or –MB engines (310R), or two 285 hp TSIO-520-B or –BB engines (T310R). In the case of the T310R, rated power was maintained up to 16,000 ft.

Maximum weights for both the 310R and T310R were: take-off 5,500 lb., landing 5,400 lb. All 310R models were fitted with three blade propellers, which had been an optional fit from the 310K onward.

The most obvious external feature of the 310R series is a 32-inch nose extension, introducing an additional baggage compartment with a 350 lb. capacity. This increased the total maximum baggage capacity to no less than 950 lb. This change is accompanied by the adoption of a shorter vertically mounted nosewheel assembly.

The other externally visible change is the deletion of the rearward ejecting exhaust augmentors below the cowlings, in favor of a conventional exhaust outlet. An adjustable cowling flap was introduced to allow cooling airflow to be adjusted dependent upon power level. Late production model aircraft were cleared for flight into known icing, provided that the appropriate ice protection system was fitted. A total of 1,332 310R/T310R were built.

An anonymous Australian-registered Cessna 310R awaiting repair after a tail strike in Queensland. The long nose, clean nacelles, raised rear window, and back-set nosewheel immediately identify this as a Cessna 310R or T310R. *Author*

The final version of Cessna 310 is the Cessna T310R. ZS-JNJ (310R-1003) was photographed at Lanseria, near Johannesburg, South Africa, shortly after the author had flown a Cessna 172 from this airfield. *Author*

The cut-away six seat cabin interior of a 1976 Cessna 310R. *Cessna Aircraft Company*

Additional Cessna 310R Images

Photographed at Hurn Airport, Bournemouth, UK, in
September 2012, N747YK is a 1975 Cessna 310R. *Jim Smith*

LN-AFB is a
Norwegian Cessna
310R or T310R
photographed at
Blackbushe,
Hampshire, UK, in
October 1991.
Jim Smith

The final and most shark-like version of the Cessna 310 was the Cessna T310R, represented here by N364NY at Henstridge, Dorset, UK, in April 2012. *Author*

The main features of the Cessna 310R are well shown in this photograph of T310R N364NY, with its long pointed nose, vertical nose leg, smooth engine cowlings with stub exhausts and cowl flaps, and clean, flowing lines. *Author*

The 1978 Cessna 310R VH-JQK shows off its distinctive lines in an attractive and artistic color scheme. It was photographed at Archerfield, Queensland, Australia, in November 2009. *Jim Smith*

Venezuelan Cessna 310R YV921P photographed at Miami Opa Locka, Florida, in December 1994. *Peter Davison*

Cyprus-registered Cessna 310R 5B-FGN photographed at
Luxembourg Findel in August 1991. *Peter Davison*

Honduras-registered Cessna 310R HR-ABB photographed
at Tegucigalpa, 2008. *Peter Davison*

Cessna 310 in Close-Up: Comparison Between Design Features

The preceding narrative discusses the evolution of the Cessna 310 through the 310R. A number of visible differences between models are mentioned in the text; these are illustrated in more detail below, together with some detailed photography of Cessna T310R N364NY taken at Henstridge, Dorset.

Fin sweep: The use of the swept fin from the Cessna 310D onward is an obvious difference and is not discussed here, being readily apparent in all the relevant photographs.

Exhaust System

The Cessna 310, 310A, and 310B featured an over-wing exhaust system in which the exhaust emerged from twin augmentor tubes forward of the wing trailing edge. This arrangement resulted in high cabin noise levels, however.

From the Cessna 310C through the Cessna 310G, the exhausts were fed through to a rectangular letter-box outlet at the wing trailing edge. The illustration compares the exhaust installation of Cessna 310B VH-REK (front) with Cessna 310C (rear), photographed at Goulburn, NSW in April 2013.

From the Cessna 310H through to the 310Q, the exhausts were relocated to pass underneath the wing, exiting to either side of the nacelle, at around mid-chord, ahead of the flap system. The accompanying photograph shows this configuration on Cessna 310Q at Sywell, in Northamptonshire.

The final exhaust configuration was introduced on the Cessna 310R, where the under-wing exhaust tubes were replaced by short exhaust stubs and adjustable cowling flaps, as seen here on N364NY.

Exhaust comparison Cessna 310B and 310C. *Author*

Revised exhaust layout for the Cessna 310H to 310Q. *Author*

Cowl flaps and stub exhausts characterize the Cessna 310R. *Author*

Tip Tanks

From the Cessna 310, through to the 310F, the aircraft made use of a rounded tip tank mounted like an end-plate at each wing tip. Each tank contained 52 US gallons, of which 50 were usable. These tanks have become generally known as "tuna-tanks' on account of their shape.

From the Cessna 310G, a sculpted upswept design was introduced, significantly changing the appearance of the whole design. The capacity of each tank remained unchanged.

General Features T310R

The following images illustrate features of the T310R N364Y that are relevant to earlier Cessna 310 models.

The rear three-quarter view below clearly shows the raised roofline and "omni-vision' rear window fitted to the 310R and to later models of the 310Q. The large cabin side window was introduced on the 310K and marketed as the "vista-view' window. The fixed footstep provides comfortable access to the wing walkway and the large starboard door that provides access to the cabin and cockpit. This feature is common to all Cessna 310 models.

Tip tank shape of early models. *Author*

Tip tank shape from Cessna 310G onward. *Author*

Access and cabin glazing of the Cessna 310R. *Author*

Baggage

The rear baggage door is just behind the starboard wing root and provides access to the main baggage compartment. This compartment is a common feature on all Cessna 310 and 320 models and has an allowable capacity of 200 lb. Access to the wing locker baggage compartments is provided by doors toward the rear of the nacelle upper surface.

These baggage compartments, with a capacity of 120 lb. on each side, were introduced on the 310I. Unique to the 310R is the 32-inch nose extension, which is provided with another baggage compartment, with a maximum capacity of 350 lb. This is accessed by a large door on the port side of the nose.

Fuselage baggage door. *Author*

The spacious fuselage baggage compartment. *Chris F. Arrington*

Access to the wing locker baggage compartment. *Author*

Extended nose baggage compartment of the Cessna 310R. *Author*

Auxiliary Wing Tanks

The sculpted wing tip tanks originated with the 310G and are fitted to all subsequent models. This photograph shows that N364Y is also fitted with auxiliary wing tanks. This is shown by the additional fuel filler on the wing inboard of the tip tank. Two options are available, providing additional usable capacity of either 40 US gallons, or 63 US gallons. This arrangement applies to both the 310Q and the 310R. Optionally, auxiliary wing locker fuel tanks can be fitted in place of the nacelle baggage compartments, with a capacity of 20 US gallons on each side.

Instrument Panel and Controls

Finally in this section, we look at the Cessna 310R instrument panel. This photograph, from Cessna Aircraft, shows the panel of a 1976 310R.

This panel features largely electromechanical gauges. Many aircraft remaining in service are likely to have been upgraded to feature glass panel displays for weather radar, GPS, and, indeed, primary flight displays.

Here, the main flight instruments—airspeed, artificial horizon, altimeter, turn and slip, gyro compass and vertical speed indicator—are grouped immediately in front of the pilot in the left seat. Below and to the left is a DME indicator; below and to the right is an exhaust gas temperature instrument. Immediately to the right of the primary flight instruments are the VOR/Glideslope and ADF radio navigation indicators and the autopilot mode selector.

The central stack contains duplicated nav/com radios, transponder and ADF controls. Just below and to the right of the latter are the flap selector and its associated position indicator. Below this are the pedestal-mounted throttle, mixture, and rpm (propeller pitch) controls. To the immediate left of this pedestal is the trim control.

Engine instruments are on the starboard side of the cockpit in front of the right seat occupant. These include manifold pressure and RPM indicators for both engines; oil pressure and temperature and cylinder head temperature for each engine; fuel quantity; alternate altimeter; and a combined fuel flow and fuel pressure gauge.

Comments on Flying and Ownership

These remarks draw upon a 1956 report in *Flight International*, "Handling the Cessna 310," and other contemporary material. The author takes these comments at face value, as he has no direct experience flying the type. The comments mainly relate to the initial production Cessna 310 and are expanded below with some comments relating to the Cessna 310Q and T310R, from Justin Cox.

Almost every review of the initial Cessna 310 comments on the high speed performance offered. With a maximum

Fuel filler caps for the main tip tank and auxiliary outboard wing tank on T310R N364Y. *Author*

The cockpit instrument panel and controls of a 1976 Cessna 310R. *Cessna Aircraft Company.*

The neat engine installation and the excellent access to the engine bay are shown in this picture of Arizona-based 1959 Cessna 310C N1722H. *Author*

speed of 218 mph and 205 mph cruise at 70% power, the overall summary is that the Cessna 310 is as fast as a Beech (Twin Bonanza) or an Aero Commander with total of 100 less hp. Climb rates of up to 1,850 ft./min are quoted. The aircraft is also praised for the excellent forward view provided.

The Cessna 310 is a very capable aircraft in terms of the combination of passenger numbers, baggage capacity, range and speed available. The cabin is wide, making the front pair of seats particularly comfortable. The passengers seated on the rear bench seat have slightly less room, however. The baggage capacity of the long-nose 310R at up to 950 lb. is particularly impressive.

Flight, in particular, was not entirely happy that the maneuver speed was as low as 159 mph, given the cruise speed above 200 mph. Even in the final production model, the T310R, the maneuver speed is as low as 170 mph, this being only 10 mph higher than the flap limiting speed.

Other sources comment that early aircraft tend to have better overall control harmony than later models, possibly due to the absence of the springs and bob-weights used in the elevator circuit of the later aircraft. There is some directional snaking in turbulent conditions, but this is improved in later aircraft with a ventral fin.

In terms of handling generally, comment is made on control friction somewhat masking the stability characteristics. The consensus seems to be of weak longitudinal stability and neutral lateral stability. The controls are also described as somewhat sloppy at low speeds. One characteristic that affects the type generally is that full tip tanks significantly increase the roll inertia and as a result, high aileron input is required to initiate and stop high roll rates when the tip tanks are full.

There appears to be a tendency for a hard landing if throttles are cut too early (particularly on the earlier short nose versions with 45 degrees maximum flap deflection). This characteristic is said to be improved on the long-nose 310R model.

The Cessna 310R and T310R offer fast, long range flying with good fuel and baggage capacities, albeit with a complex fuel system. ZS-JNJ was photographed at Lanseria, South Africa. *Author*

Sleek and purposeful, VH-REK is a 1957 Cessna 310B photographed at Goulburn, NSW, Australia, in the ownership of the Historic Aircraft Restoration Society. *Author*

Moving away from handling qualities, there is general agreement that the over-wing exhausts of the early models result in high cabin noise levels. There is also some criticism of the single starboard entry door that requires passengers to "clamber' into the rear seats.

A common criticism is that the nosewheel assembly is not particularly robust, at least on the earlier models. Problems are avoided with regular maintenance and inspection; preferably, the pilot should avoid heavy braking while turning on the ground.

The early models have a simple fuel system, with only the two wing tip tanks. Later models can have both wing auxiliary tanks and wing locker tanks, which makes fuel management more complex.

The Type Certificate Data Sheet lists the cockpit placards that make the procedure quite clear. The extract below actually relates to the Cessna 340, but is also valid for Cessna 310 with the equivalent tank configuration.

"SET FUEL SELECTOR VALVES TO LEFT MAIN TANK FOR LEFT ENGINE AND RIGHT MAIN TANK FOR RIGHT ENGINE IN TAKEOFF, LANDING, EMERGENCY AND FIRST 60 MIN. OF FLIGHT" (first 60 minutes with 40 gallon auxiliary tank; first 90 minutes of flight with optional 63 gallon auxiliary tank)

If optional wing locker tanks are installed: "OPERATE ON MAIN TANKS UNTIL FUEL QUANTITY IS LESS THAN 180 LB. PER TANK" then:

"TRANSFER WING LOCKER FUEL WHILE OPERATING ON MAIN TANKS IN STRAIGHT AND LEVEL FLIGHT"; "TURN TRANSFER PUMPS OFF WHEN LIGHTS ILLUMINATE"; and "SWITCH TO AUXILIARY TANKS WHEN MAIN FUEL IS AGAIN LESS THAN 180 LB. PER TANK"

The wing locker tanks can only cross-feed to the mains and do not directly feed the engines, so the procedure is to wait until there is available capacity in the main tanks before transferring fuel from the wing lockers, then wait again for the tip tanks to have adequate unused capacity before using the auxiliary tank fuel. The flight would then be completed using the remaining fuel in the main (wingtip) tanks.

Even when flying the aircraft regularly, the pilot flying an aircraft fitted with both auxiliary wing tanks and wing locker tanks will need methodical procedures and a good mental picture of the fuel state as the flight continues.

With all these tanks fitted, there are a fair number of fuel drains/vents to be checked. The height of the tip tanks can also make checking their content levels awkward.

LV-ITF is a less-than pristine Cessna 310K photographed at Morena, Buenos Aires, Argentina, in October 2012. *Peter Davidson*

This view of T310R N364NY at Henstridge, Dorset, UK, emphasizes the clean design and characteristic features of the T310R, final production model of the Cessna 310 series. *Author*

A beautiful 1980 Cessna 310R VH-LGC (310R-1827)
photographed in January 2009 at Bankstown, Sydney,
NSW, Australia. *Jim Smith*

Justin Cox has experience regularly flying Cessna 310Q G-AYND from Bournemouth to northern France, typically to Dijon, or Le Bourget, Paris. On first being asked to fly the aircraft, Justin asked for a check ride to help with understanding fuel management. In the event, he flew some circuits and had a careful telephone briefing from the pilot who had been routinely flying the aircraft, concerning fuel management.

G-AYND was fitted with wing auxiliary tanks, but did not have wing locker tanks. The briefing indicated that the aircraft should be flown on the mains (tip tanks) for sixty minutes before using the wing tanks. It was stressed that the wing tanks should not be used for more than forty-four minutes (a surprisingly precise number).

On the following trip to France, Justin was timing his usage of these tanks while flying IFR at 7,000 ft. Just past forty-four minutes of use, he was approaching the French coast when the port engine stopped, followed, only seconds later, by the starboard engine. Rapidly selecting the mains and the fuel pumps, both engines were quickly re-started. This is an experience that one only wants to have once!

Other than this incident, Justin is generally impressed by the Cessna 310. It gives the impression of good, solid, predictable characteristics and generous cabin volume and baggage capacity. In particular, it is a smooth and stable IFR platform.

The later models such as the 310R have bob weights and springs in the elevator circuit to achieve the necessary aft CG range and for longitudinal stability. This, combined with the increased pitch inertia of the lengthened fuselage, tends to result in the 310R being somewhat heavy in pitch at all speeds. Turbocharged aircraft require careful throttle management to avoid shock cooling the turbos in the descent.

Justin comments that, "the Cessna 310 is second in my opinion only to the Beech Baron, which is a real pilot's aircraft, although it does have a smaller cabin." Both aircraft are, in his opinion, easier to fly than the Twin Comanche which is, in his opinion, "the hardest to land properly."

Specials

As with many long-lived and successful designs, there are a number of after-market improvements available for the Cessna 310. Many of these options are characterized by installing higher power engines in combination with various aerodynamic modifications to improve performance. Examples of such modifications include a range of variants from Colemill Enterprises of Nashville and similar adaptations from RAM Aircraft of Waco, Texas.

The Colemill adaptations are applied to non-turbo models up to the 310Q and typically feature engine power increases to 285 hp or 300 hp per side, with corresponding performance improvements, particularly in take-off run and climb rates.

RAM offers broadly equivalent enhancements for turbo-charged models at either 300 hp or 325 hp (RAM IV) per side. The RAM modifications also allow an increase in take-off weight by 170 lb. to 5,670 lb. The RAM IV has a quoted 75% cruise speed of an impressive 243 kt at 18,000 ft. and climb rates approaching 3,000 ft./min. Despite the significant range of modifications involved, there is often little to distinguish RAM-modified aircraft from the normal production aircraft, other than, perhaps, a discreet logo on the fuselage side or engine cowling.

Rather than dwell on these upgrades in detail, two significant variants are discussed in more detail below, these being the 1961 Riley 65 and an example of a 310R modified by R/STOL for short field performance and low speed handling.

There is often little external indication that an aircraft has been upgraded. This is the RAM logo on the engine cowling of Cessna 320F N21MT.
Chris Arrington

Riley 65

The first special variant of the Cessna 310 to be marketed was the high performance Riley 65 and its related developments, the Riley Rocket, Turbostream, and Super 310. Jack M. Riley purchased a number of Cessna 310 aircraft and modified them to such an extent that they were marketed as a separate type. Jack M. Riley Jr. was later to head Administration and Engineering for RAM Aircraft. Structural modifications were introduced to strengthen the type, reflecting the higher performance available.

The comments below reflect a *Flight International* article from September 1961 and additional material from *Jane's All the World's Aircraft*.

The most evident and externally visible change for the Riley 65 was to replace Cessna's over-wing augmentor exhaust system with a system fitted below each engine nacelle. The other distinguishing features of the type were an additional third window on each side at the rear of the cabin and the introduction of a one-piece windscreen. Twenty US gallon auxiliary tanks were installed in the rear of each engine nacelle.

The Riley 65 was a contemporary of Cessna's 310D, which was fitted with 260 hp engines. The Riley 65 was offered with either 240 hp (O-470-D) or 260 hp (IO-470-M) engines. There was a great emphasis on quality of finish and this was reflected in higher cruising speeds. Maximum take-off weight was 4,830 lb. and an empty weight of 3,000 lb. was quoted.

The UK distributor Keegan Aviation claimed that the 240 hp Riley 65 had similar performance to the 260 hp 310D. This was backed up with a cruise speed of 225 mph at 75% power; slightly faster than that of the more pow-

The cleaned-up Riley 65 can be recognized by its under-wing exhausts and additional rear window. G-ARTK was photographed at the Biggin Hill Air Fair, Keny, UK, in May 1973. This aircraft was imported by dealers Keegan Aviation in 1961.
Barry Collman

Riley 65 OY-DRH photographed at Hanover Langenhagen, Germany, in May 1978. It was built in 1956 and was previously registered as N5207A and G-ASSZ.
Ad Vercruijsse

erful 260 hp 310D. The 260 hp Riley model was 10 mph faster again. A climb rate of 1,800 ft./min was quoted. The UK sales price was, surprisingly, significantly less than that of the 310D.

An eye catching sales slogan was that the Riley 65 could, "fly faster on one engine than a Piper Apache on two." The under-wing exhausts resulted in a much quieter cabin, assisted by the use of sound absorbing materials in the cabin.

The Riley 65 was followed by the Riley Rocket with two 290 hp IO-540-A1A5 engines and an increase in fuel volume to 168 US gallons. The additional power increased the 75% power cruise speed to 250 mph and 232 mph could be achieved at 50% power at 10,000 ft. The Turbo-Rocket used two 310 hp TIO-540-A2C engines with a quoted cruise speed of 300 mph at 20,000 ft.

The final Riley Super 310 had a similar specification, but used the 310 hp Continental TSIO-520-J and was applicable to both Cessna 310 and 320 models up to the T310R and 320F. The quoted cruising speed for this model at 24,000 ft. was 294 mph.

Cessna 310R R/STOL

James L. Robertson pioneered the development of short take-off and landing (STOL) modifications for single and twin engine American general aviation aircraft from Beechcraft, Cessna and Piper. These kits were sold through the Robertson Aircraft Corporation.

In 1985, R/STOL Systems Inc. of Raleigh, Durham, North Carolina, took over the Robertson assets and continued marketing STOL packages for a very wide range of aircraft. This activity was taken over by Sierra Industries of Uvalde, Texas, in September 1986.

These modifications are most notable for the replacement of the original flap systems (split flaps in the case of the Cessna 310) with large Fowler flaps that increase the wing area as they are extended. Dependent

The large, area increasing Fowler flaps of this R/STOL-modified 1962 Cessna 310R N419PD are shown prominently in this image. With full fuel (163 US gallons) a payload of 852 lb. is available. *Jerry Temple Aviation*

The R/STOL modifications to N419PD include both Fowler Flaps and vortex generators, allowing a maximum weight increase from 5,500 to 5,680 lb. This aircraft cruises at 175 kt TAS and has weather radar and de-icing and anti-icing equipment. *Jerry Temple Aviation*

on the type, additional modifications can include drooping ailerons; spoiler systems for low speed roll control; chordwise fences on the upper wing at the junction between the flaps and ailerons; a double-hinged rudder; automatic trim change with flap deflection and various other aerodynamic fixes.

The aircraft featured here is a 1976 Cessna 310R N419PD with R/STOL modifications, being sold by Cessna twin specialist, Jerry Temple Aviation Inc.

This aircraft features the large R/STOL Fowler flaps, leading edge cuffs, airflow vanes on the engine nacelles and the wing root, and wing vortex generators. These modifications permit a weight increase to 5,680 lb. (from 5,500 lb.). This aircraft is also fitted with de-ice and anti-ice systems and an extensive avionics equipment package including: Garmin 530W com/nav/GPS/map, Bendix RDR-150 radar, Collins 2nd nav/com, and Cessna 400B autopilot. The empty weight is 3,850 lb., providing a payload of 853 lb. with the 163 US gallon full fuel load.

Comparative data from R/STOL and Sierra indicate a reduction in minimum single engine control airspeed of around 16 kt and a stalling speed below 65 kt.

Cessna 320 Skyknight

From 1962 to 1968, Cessna manufactured a high altitude turbo-charged six seat variant of the Cessna 310, the Cessna 320 Skyknight.

The name reflected contemporary practice at Cessna, which had within its family of aircraft the 172 Skyhawk, 175 Skylark, 182 Skylane, 185 Skywagon, the 205 and 206 Super Skywagon, and the 336 Skymaster. After 1968, the Skyknight was effectively superseded by the T310P through to T310R.

1962 Cessna 320

The 1962 first production model was the 320 Skyknight. This resembled a 310F with an extra cabin window, giving four windows on each side. The prototype was N34262 and type approval was gained on 24 May 1961. The initial 1962 production model was the only 320 variant to retain un-canted tip tanks, these being introduced on the 1962 310G and used on subsequent 320 models.

Power was provided by two 260 hp Continental TSIO-470-B engines with a rated altitude of 16,000 ft. Another externally distinguishing feature was the use of modified nacelles with louvers to improve cooling at high altitude. The main performance benefit came from the ability to cruise at high altitude, providing that oxygen equipment

G-ARYU is the first Cessna 320 to be imported into the UK and was photographed at Blackbushe, Hampshire. *Jim Smith*

was used. The air intake for the turbochargers was provided in the leading edge of the wing roots.

As with other turbocharged aircraft, there was a need for careful engine management to avoid shock cooling either the engines or the turbochargers in the descent. It was also necessary to keep the engines running after flight, while the supercharger turbines spun down.

The specification included a maximum take-off weight of 4,990 lb. with a maximum landing weight of 4,750 lb. A cruising speed of 244 mph was quoted at 75% power and

The 1962 Cessna 320 offered six seats and turbocharged engines permitting high altitude operation. N5411E (c/n 635) is one of the prototypes used for initial publicity work. *Cessna Aircraft Company*

The initial Cessna 320 model is distinguished by the use of the early Cessna 310 wing tip tank design. N5783X was photographed at Manassas, Virginia, in December 1989. *Jim Smith*

Cessna 320 N5769X seen at John Wayne Airport, Orange County, California. *Author*

24,000 ft. Key limit speeds included flap and gear limits of 140 mph and maneuvering speed 167 mph.

Fuel capacity was 100 US gallons (usable) in the tip tanks, although optional wing auxiliary tanks could be fitted to raise the maximum capacity to 133 US gallons. The baggage capacity was 200 lb. A total of 110 Cessna 320s were built.

This air to air photograph shows the pleasing maroon, beige, and white colour scheme of N5411E. *Cessna Aircraft Company*

The additional side windows that distinguish all Cessna 320 variants are clearly shown in this picture of N5411E taxying. Models up to the Cessna 320C also featured engine nacelle cooling louvers. *Cessna Aircraft Company*

Later Models: 320A to 320F

From 1963 onward, a new letter suffix to the designation indicated the model year. The 320A, which was granted type approval on 10 May 1962, introduced canted stabila-tip tanks. The maximum take-off and landing weight was increased to 5,200 lb. The baggage capacity was increased to a total of 420 lb. A total of forty-seven 320As were built.

The 1964 320B added extended nacelles with wing baggage lockers providing an additional 120 lb. per side to provide a total baggage capacity of 600 lb. The maximum flap travel was reduced from 45 to 35 degrees. Type approval was granted on May 16, 1963, and a total of sixty-two were built.

The 1965 320C was essentially identical in appearance to the previous year's model and featured a fifteen-inch longer cabin (to provide an optional seventh seat). The baggage capacity remained 600 lb. Type approval was granted on April 24, 1964, and a total of seventy-three 320C were built.

From 1963, the Cessna 320A introduced canted tip tanks. CF-QAD was photographed at a snowy Biggin Hill, Kent, UK. *Author*

N9840L is a 1963 Cessna 320B with extended nacelle baggage lockers. *Author*

N1000K is a Cessna 320D Executive Skynight. This model introduced a revised rear window shape and a cleaner cowling line, similar to that of the Cessna 310R. *Author*

The 1966 320D model was called the Executive Skyknight. Power was provided by two 285 hp TSIO-520-B, with a rated altitude of 16,000 ft. This, and subsequent models featured a change in rear cabin window shape. The cowling shape was also modified with cowl flaps replacing the characteristic vents on the lower cowlings of the earlier models.

The quoted maximum speed for this model was 275 mph with a 75% power cruise speed at 20,000 ft. of 261 mph. The fuel capacity was increased by 10 US gallons with use of larger 20.5 US gallon auxiliary tanks on each side. Type approval was granted on April 9, 1965, and 130 320Ds were built.

The 1967 320E featured a 100 lb. increase in take-off and landing weight to 5,300 lb. Distinguishing features included a pointed nose and a single piece windshield. Less visible changes included a modified undercarriage and new ailerons. The undercarriage and flap limit speeds were increased to 160 mph.

As with other models in the Cessna 300 family, there was a range of fuel capacity options, dependent upon the combination of auxiliary tanks fitted.

Briefly, the options were as follows:

1. Two tip tanks with total usable capacity of 100 US gallons, plus
2. An optional additional two 20.5 gallon wing tanks (143 US gallon total)
3. The option of a further two optional wing locker tanks (of 20 gal. each) (providing a total fuel capacity of 183 US gallons). When these wing locker transfer tanks are fitted, the capacity of the wing baggage lockers is limited to 40 lb. on each side.

Type approval was granted on July 26, 1966, and 110 320Es were built.

The final model was the 1968 320F Executive Skyknight, which featured mostly minor changes compared with the previous model. Type approval was granted on May 10, 1967, and forty-five 320Fs were built.

Utah-based N3491Q is a Cessna 320E. *Author*

Cessna 320E N320AR taxies after arrival at Oshkosh, Wisconsin, in 1985. *Author*

The refined final version of the Cessna 320, N21MT is a Cessna 320F Executive Skynight. *Chris Arrington*

Cessna 320 Gallery

Cessna 320A CF-QAD at Biggin Hill, Kent, UK. *Author*

An unidentified Cessna 320 (320A to 320C) at Oshkosh, Wisconsin. *Author*

The refined grey leather interior and panel of Cessna 320F N21MT. *Chris Arrington*

Cessna 340

In 1962, Cessna flew the prototype Cessna 411 cabin class business twin. In this context, "cabin-class" meant that the aircraft was entered via an in-built airstair door, with the passengers seated in individual seats on either side of an aisle.

There followed a range of related models of the Cessna 400 series, including the pressurized Cessna 421 and 414, which entered production in 1970. These are described in more detail in Section B of this book.

Shortly thereafter, the C340 entry-level pressurized twin was launched, receiving type approval on October 15, 1971. The Cessna 340 used the wing of the Cessna 414, together with a Cessna 310-based empennage married to a new pressurized fuselage.

The fuselage featured four elliptical windows on each side and offered a pressure differential of 4.2 lb./sq. in., providing an 8,000 ft. cabin height at 20,000 ft. flight altitude. The Cessna 340 offered the ability to fly in comfort above weather without recourse to oxygen masks. (Above 23,500 ft., oxygen is required up to a maximum operating altitude of 30,000 ft.). Many aircraft are fitted with anti-ice and de-ice equipment to add further flexibility to flight planning.

Cessna's first "cabin class" twin was the Cessna 411, which first flew in 1962. N411PM (complete with wrinkled rudder) is a Cessna 411A, photographed at Terrill, Texas. *Author*

The uniquely 1970s cabin interior of a Cessna 340. *Cessna Aircraft Company*

A dramatic publicity photograph of N4135G against an impressive skyscape. *Cessna Aircraft Company*

Somewhat surprisingly to the layman, the Cessna 340 was certificated on the same type certificate as the Cessna 320.

Power for the 340 was provided by a pair of 285 hp Continental TSIO-520-K or –520-KB engines with a rated altitude of 16,000 ft. The maximum gross weight was 5,975 lb. and Cessna quoted an empty weight of 3,725 lb., although a figure of 3,900 lb. might be more representative of a fully equipped aircraft.

Large fuel and baggage capacities were provided to make the aircraft suitable for a range of business and pleasure uses. The fuel capacity is up to 203 US gallons in tip tanks, with optional auxiliary tanks (which offer either 40 or 63 gallons usable), and wing locker tanks (20 gallons each side).

Baggage can be carried in a nose compartment, a fuselage baggage bay and wing lockers in the rear of one, or both, engine nacelles. The total capacity provided is up to 930 lb., of which 240 lb. can be carried in the wing lockers, 340 lb. in the fuselage bay, and 350 lb. in the nose compartment.

The slight disadvantage of all this capacity is the need to take care over weight and balance. With six occupants and no baggage and a 3,900 lb. empty weight, the maximum fuel load would be around 1,035 lb., compared to the maximum capacity of 1,218 lb. At the Cessna-quoted empty weight, it would just be possible to fly with six occupants and full fuel, albeit with no baggage.

Cessna 340A G-ENAM on the approach to land at Cranfield, Bedfordshire, UK. This model had increased power and take-off weight. *Author*

N4146G, a Cessna 340 on display at the EAA AirVenture fly-in at Oshkosh, Wisconsin. *Author*

Swiss registered Cessna 340A HB-LPK at the Royal International Air Tattoo, Cottesmore, Norfolk, UK, in July 2000. *Author*

N2668Y is a Cessna 340 seen at McCarran International Airport, Las Vegas, Nevada in February 1981. *Author*

A realistic cruising speed of around 200 kt can be achieved at 75% power at 20,000 ft. A total of 350 Cessna 340s were built between 1972 and 1975.

An upgraded model, the Cessna 340A, was produced from 1976, having received type approval on November 19, 1975. The 340A was powered by two 310 hp Continental TSIO-520-N or -520-NB engines with 20,000 ft. rated altitude. Maximum take-off weight was increased by 15 lb. to 5,990 lb. The increased power translates to a speed increase of around 15 kt compared to the C340 at comparable altitudes and power settings.

The Cessna 340A was sold in greater numbers than the previous model. A total of 948 340As were constructed between 1976 and 1984.

A review of available comments on the type has produced the following reasonably widely held views.

On the positive side, the type is seen as providing:

• Excellent value for money in terms of pressurized comfort and performance
• Straightforward responsive handling with no vices
• Good control capability with one engine out

The main concerns are as follows:
• Limited payload capacity with full fuel
• The narrow access from cockpit to cabin
• The need to avoid shock cooling either the engines or turbochargers in descent, particularly when slowing down to the relatively low undercarriage limit speed of 140 kt. This speed restriction can make it harder to fit the type into a landing sequence of faster commercial aircraft.

VH-PTO is a Cessna 340A photographed at Parrafield, SA, Australia, in 2006. *Jim Smith*

D-IMHW is a Cessna 340A at Blackbushe, Hampshire, UK. Close inspection shows that this aircraft is equipped with a wing vortex generator kit. *Author*

VH-CIO is an upgraded RAM Series VII aircraft with 335 hp on each side. This aircraft is also fitted with a vortex generator kit. It was photographed at Archerfield, QLD, Australia, in November 2008. *Jim Smith*

Having criticized the type for its comparatively modest load capability, it is important to note that this is not the end of the story.

There is a range of after-market upgrades available, particularly from RAM Aircraft. The RAM IV increases power available to 325 hp per side, with the RAM VI and VII offering two 335 hp engines.

There is a vortex generator kit, which has been widely adopted, as it permits no less than a 300 lb. increase in take-off weight to 6,290 lb., most of which is immediately available as disposable load.

Other upgraded models are available from Riley (the Super 340 and Rocket 340) and short take-off and landing variants from Robertson/Sierra Industries.

The Riley Super 340 is broadly equivalent to a Cessna 340A, using 310 hp Continental TSIO-520-N engines in place of the standard Cessna 340 285 hp engines. The type was certificated in 1974 and a significant number of Cessna 340 aircraft have been modified to this standard. The Rocket 340 uses 340 hp TSIO-540-R engines driving counter-rotating propellers. A 65% power cruising speed at 24,000 ft. of 240 kt is quoted for this variant.

Riley also marketed a turboprop Cessna 340 derivative, the Riley Jet Prop 340 powered by two flat-rated LTP 101 engines and offering a maximum take-off weight of 5,990 lb.

N125 is another modified example, in this case a Riley Super 340 with two 310 hp engines (equivalent to the Cessna 340A fit) replacing the standard 285 hp engines. The aircraft was photographed at Washington National (Ronald Reagan) Airport, DC. *Author*

D-ILWA is an R/STOL Cessna 340A III photographed at Cranfield, Bedfordshire, UK, in July 1995. Only the external flap tracks beneath the wing trailing edge indicate that this is a STOL-modified aircraft. *Jim Smith*

Cessna 340 Gallery

Venezuelan Cessna 340 YV370T photographed at
Chalareve, Caracas, Venezuela, in 2011. *Peter Davison*

A Venezuelan Cessna 340 YV2337 seen at Chalareve, Caracas, Venezuela, in 2011. *Peter Davison*

Cessna 335

The final model in this family is the Cessna 335. This type, which received its type approval on October 2, 1979, was a lower price unpressurized version of the C340A. The C335 was powered by two 300 hp Continental TSIO-520-EB engines, with a maximum take-off weight of 5,990 lb. The type is otherwise identical to Cessna 340A, from which it is also externally indistinguishable. This was a far less successful proposition, and only sixty-five were built, all of them in 1980.

A 1980 Cessna 335 N36N, being offered for sale by Jerry Temple Aviation. This aircraft has vortex generators and a 1,827 lb. useful load (empty 4,463 lb., gross 6290 lb.); it offers a 182 kt cruise speed at 65% power. *Jerry Temple Aviation*

Cessna 335 II N2709R photographed in 1995, in Arizona. This is an unpressurized version to the Cessna 340, to which it is externally identical; only sixty-five Cessna 335s were built. *Author*

A Venezuelan Cessna 335 YV1505 at Fort Lauderdale, Florida in 2012. *Peter Davison*

N6595C is a RAM-modified 1980 Cessna 335 fitted with vortex generators and an extensive avionics fit. Its empty weight is 3,963 lb., gross weight 5,990 lb., providing a disposable load of 2,027 lb. Maximum fuel is 147 US gallons giving a payload with full fuel of 1,169 lb. (passengers plus baggage). *Joe Renda: Bay Air Aircraft Sales*

Cessna 303 and T303 Clipper/Crusader

During the late 1970s, Cessna's main competitors, Piper and Beechcraft, introduced new entry-level retractable undercarriage twin engine aircraft, respectively the PA-44 Seminole and the Beechcraft 76 Duchess.

Cessna responded with the announcement in February 1978 of a new four seat design, the Cessna 303. It is widely stated that the prototype N303CP flew for the first time on February 14, 1978, although the image caption provided by Cessna Aircraft indicates that the first flight took place the following day, flown by test pilot Bruce Barrett.

The 303 was a slightly inelegant looking twin, powered by two 160 hp Lycoming engines and having a take-off weight of 3,600 lb. Uniquely for Cessna, the type featured a cruciform empennage with the tailplane mounted partway up the fin.

Cessna, having reviewed the marketplace and the number of competitors in this class, which now also included the Grumman American GA-7 Cougar, decided to significantly re-think the Cessna 303 design.

The type that emerged to enter production was the Cessna T303, initially known as the Clipper and later renamed Crusader. Flown for the first time on October 17, 1979, this was a six seat cabin-class aircraft powered by two 250 hp turbocharged Continental TSIO-520-AE engines, driving counter-rotating propellers. Rated power is achieved at 15,000 ft. and a cruising speed of some 193 kt is quoted at 71% power and 20,000 ft.

The prototype Cessna T303 Clipper flown by Tom Wallace during its first flight on October 17, 1979. The type was later renamed the Cessna Crusader. *Cessna Aircraft Company*

Eight out of the twelve Cessna T303 then on the British register gather for a fly-in at Cambridge Airport, UK, in September 2004. *Roche Bentley*

N303CP, the prototype of the original four-seat Cessna 303, flies for the first time over the winter Wichita landscape on February 15, 1978. *Cessna Aircraft Company*

The T303 maximum take-off weight was 5,150 lb. with landing weight 5,000 lb. (which could be increased to 5,150 lb. when fitted with optional heavy duty wheels and brakes). A high landing gear extension speed of 175 kt was provided, overcoming one of the operational criticisms of the Cessna 340. Once down, the undercarriage can remain extended up to the aircraft's never exceed speed of 210 kt.

Type approval for the modified design was received on August 24, 1981, and the type was, in effect, a lighter replacement for the commercially unsuccessful and heavier, higher power, Cessna 335.

The fuel system was simplified compared with earlier models, to provide 153 US gallons of usable fuel, divided between two integral wing tanks. The baggage capacity was a total of 590 lb., distributed between nose bay, fuselage, and wing locker compartments.

Maximum flap deflection was 30 degrees, a lower figure than Cessna had used on earlier types. The first stage of flap can be selected at 175 kt, with full flap limited to 125 kt.

Cessna quoted an empty weight of 3,364 lb., giving a disposable load of 1,786 lb. With a maximum fuel load of 918 lb., the weight available for occupants and their baggage

Cessna T303 G-PUSI gets airborne from its home base of Henstridge, Dorset, UK, in April 2012. *Author*

is 868 lb. With an enhanced avionics package and a more representative empty weight of around 3,500 lb., this will be restricted to a lower figure. As with other Cessna twins, weight and balance calculations form a necessary part of flight planning.

T303 G-PUSI retracts its undercarriage against a dramatic cloud backdrop on August 28, 2010. *Author*

A total of 315 Cessna T303 were built in a relatively short production run with deliveries from 1982 to 1984. The TCDS lists serial numbers of twenty-six individual aircraft that are "not eligible for US Airworthiness Certificates."

Reports from owners and operators uniformly praise the excellent handing qualities and control harmony of the T303. The excellent handling may, in part, be attributed to the lack of springs and bob weights in the elevator circuit; these are a prominent feature of both the Cessna 310 and 320 series. The cockpit layout and equipment accessibility is also praised.

One aspect commented on is that a firm pull is required to achieve rotation on take-off, with a concomitant risk of over-rotation. A tendency to Dutch roll in turbulence is also reported.

Some personal observations on flying and owning the type have been provided by Roche Bentley, owner of G-ROCH. Roche has owned this aircraft since 1990, buying it from Miller Aviation in Johnson City, New York. Miller Aviation

runs a business aviation charter service, also using the aircraft, and were using the aircraft for training and instrument rating renewals and so on. Roche had the aircraft ferried back to the UK at a cost of around $5,000 and at the time of writing now has 960 hours on the T303.

Roche's comments are as follows:

"It is very easy and forgiving to fly and not complicated to operate. The cabin and built-in airstair make it like a mini-King Air, with a feel of interior space and comfort. The children were very happy in the cabin, but preferred to use headsets to keep the noise levels down.

"With a house in Brittany, we fly there several times a year and, after clearing customs, land at Dinan, where there is a small, very welcoming club. The T303 is very good on a grass runway due to the combination of good performance and a smooth, forgiving undercarriage.

Cessna T303
G-ROCH at Main Hall
Farm,
Cambridgeshire, UK.
Roche Bentley

Experience on many strips in France and the UK has shown that basically, you can take a T303 almost anywhere that you can land a Cessna 172.

"Performance is good and we cruise at 145 kt using around 100 liters (27 US gallons) an hour. My typical heights are just below airways, as its weight of 2,336 kg (5,150 lb) makes it liable for Eurocontrol en route charges. As a result, we rarely fly IFR, but the aircraft flies beautifully in IMC. The Bendix radar and Garmin 530 provide storm avoidance and easy navigation."

Roche has flown the aircraft on one engine on all his currency checks and instrument rating renewals, but has never experienced a failure in flight. He reports that the aircraft will climb positively, albeit relatively slowly, provided the airspeed is correct.

Baggage capacity is excellent and permits six adults with six half sets of golf clubs and weekend bags. The engine pods will take two half sets each and the remaining baggage goes in the nose bay or to the rear.

Roche has taken his T303 through France and Spain, and to the islands of Sardinia, Corfu, and Crete. A particularly

Roche Bentley and his T303 at Dinard, en route to Merlins over Malta in September 2005. *Roche Bentley*

Cessna T303 G-ROCH at Dinan, Brittany, France. *Roche Bentley*

fond memory was acting as the air support aircraft for a Spitfire and Hurricane that flew down to Malta for an event called Merlins over Malta. He comments, "the T303 performed perfectly and I loved flying it in formation with a warbird on each wingtip."

One downside of ownership is that at more than thirty years old, one has to be prepared for the replacement of worn out parts; regular use and keen maintenance are the keys to reliability. There are a few recommended and mandatory checks that have been promulgated by Cessna, but these are not onerous and can be completed during an annual check.

Most owners love their aircraft and only part with them in response to a failed medical, although the high cost of overpriced avgas may also be a factor. Roche comments that, "at present (2012) prices for well-kept T303s appear to be somewhat higher in the United States than in Europe." Dependent on ferry costs, therefore, a European owner might find it attractive to sell their aircraft in the United States.

Supermarine Spitfire Vb G-MKVB BM597 flies off the starboard wing tip of G-ROCH. *Merlins over Malta*

Canadian-built Hurricane G-HURI "Z5140" photographed from the supporting Cessna T303 en route to Merlins over Malta in September 2005. *Merlins over Malta*

Cessna T303 Gallery

G-ROCH on the sunlit apron of Shoreham Airport, West Sussex, UK. *Roche Bentley*

Owner Peter Drew shows off the extra-large cargo door fitted to his Cessna T303 G-OAPE. *Roche Bentley*

The instrument panel of G-OAPE shows large, easily readable, and well laid-out instruments and displays. *Roche Bentley*

Cessna T303 YS-303-P at Ilopango, San Salvador, El Salvador, in 2011. *Peter Davison*

Part B: Cessna 400 Series

The production of the various aircraft within the Cessna 400 series overlapped in time and the various types are presented in the order of each type's first flight date. The overall timelines for the production of the Cessna 400 series are also shown.

The Cessna 400 series is made up of a number of closely related types, many of which were produced in parallel to each other.

The initial model of cabin-class twin was the Cessna 411, which first flew in 1962, with a production run lasting from 1965 to 1986. This was followed by the near simultaneous introduction of the Cessna 401 (produced from 1967 to 1972), 402, and 421 (both built from 1967 to 1981). A sub-variant of the Cessna 421, the Cessna 414, was produced from 1970 through to 1986.

A larger air taxi version derived from the Cessna 402, the Cessna 404, was flown in 1975 and produced from 1977 until 1982. A further new model, the turbine-powered Cessna 441 Conquest commuter liner was developed and manufactured from 1975 to 1987. A turboprop development of the Cessna 421, the

TIMELINES FOR MODELS
within the Cessna 400 series

C414
1970-86

C421
1967-81

C402
1967-81

1960

1970

C401
1967-72

C411
1962

A 1965 photograph of the Cessna 411, Cessna's first "cabin class" twin.
Cessna Aircraft Company

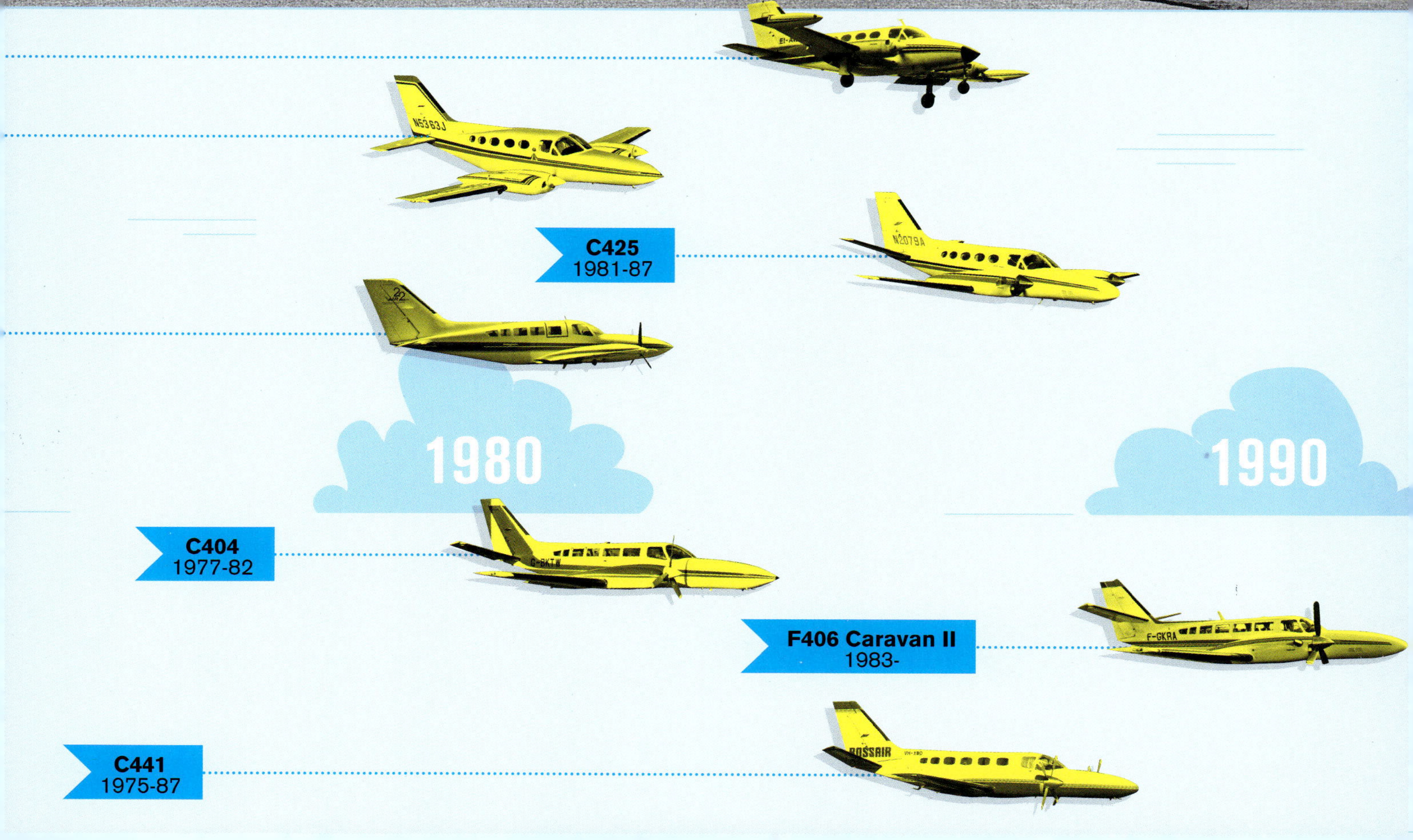

C425
1981-87

C404
1977-82

F406 Caravan II
1983-

C441
1975-87

1980

1990

Cessna 425, was introduced in 1981 and produced until 1987. This type was initially marketed as the Corsair and later as the Conquest I, the Cessna 441 then becoming the Conquest II.

Finally, a license was agreed with Reims Aviation for the production of a turbine derivative of the Cessna 404 in France. This aircraft, which entered production in 1983, was designated the Reims F406 Caravan II.

The above description determines the sequence in which the various types are discussed below.

Overview, Origins, and Competition

In the early 1960s, the Cessna 310 and 320 were doing a great job in providing high performance twin engine aircraft for the private owner. Cessna realized, however, that there was a significant market for "cabin class" commercial twins; aircraft with integral air stairs for their passengers and a passenger cabin separated from the cockpit, with seats provided either side of a central aisle. This configuration was well suited to executive and air taxi use, a market that could not be addressed by the Cessna 310 and 320.

The outstanding aircraft in this class was the Beech Queen Air, which had been flown in August 1958. Cessna flew the prototype of its Cessna 411 on July 18, 1962, with a view to competing with the Beechcraft Queen Air.

By January 1964, Beechcraft had flown the prototype of a pressurized turbine-powered derivative of the Queen Air, which was the enormously successful King Air—a type whose derivatives remain in production today.

Piper also entered this marketplace with the PA-31 Navajo, first flown in September 1964. Aero Commander continued with the progressive development of its model range, with stretched versions including the Grand Commander (1962) and the Turbo Commander (1964).

The Beechcraft Queen Air flew for the first time in August 1958 and was well-established in the marketplace by the time the Cessna 411 was launched. *Author*

Aero Commander continued development of its twin engine high wing range, later models including the Grand Commander (1962) and the turboprop Turbo Commander (1964). *Author*

The pressurized turboprop Beechcraft King Air was flown in January 1964 and was enormously successful, with derivatives still being manufactured in 2016. *Author*

Piper also recognized the value of a cabin class twin. Its PA-31 Navajo was first flown in 1964. *Author*

Cessna 411 and 411A

The Cessna 411 was an unpressurized six to eight seat low wing monoplane, with Cessna's trademark "stabila-tip' wingtip-mounted fuel tanks. An integral airstair door was fitted to allow passengers to enter the cabin. Power was provided by two 340 hp geared and supercharged six cylinder Continental GTSIO-540-C engines driving three blade propellers, and delivering their rated power up 16,000 ft. critical altitude.

The Cessna 411 received its FAA type approval on August 17, 1964, with production deliveries beginning in early 1965. An improved version, the Cessna 411A received approval on January 26, 1967. A total of 300 Cessna 411s had been built when production stopped in 1968, of these, 250 were Cessna 411s, the remainder being C411As.

The type was criticized early in its life for difficult handling characteristics with one engine failed, causing its certification to be reviewed by the FAA. This confirmed that the aircraft met all the required standards. The rudder force with one engine out was close to the maximum allowed and the failed engine needed to be cleaned up promptly (propeller feathered and cooling doors closed) to maximize performance with one engine out.

G-AWDJ is a Cessna 411, photographed at London Heathrow Airport in mid-1970. *Author*

Cessna 411A N3252R was photographed by Cessna Aircraft in 1967 for publicity purposes. *Cessna Aircraft Company*

Cessna 411A N3285R at McCarran International Airport, Las Vegas, Nevada, in February 1981. *Author*

One widely available after-market modification is the fitting of a vortex generator kit, which is widely reported to improve single engine handling significantly.

The wingspan is 39 ft. 10^1/$_4$ in. and maximum weight for take-off and landing is 6,500 lb. A typical cruising speed at 10,000 ft. is quoted as 195 kt. The main difference between the Cessna 411 and 411A is that the latter offers increased baggage capacity, although this model also features a number of other minor improvements. Baggage allowance for the 411A is increased from 700 lb. to 930 lb., due to increased capacity in the nose baggage compartment.

Standard fuel capacity comprised two tip tanks with 50 US gal. usable each, and two wing tanks, each with 36.5 US gas usable, for a total of 173 US gal. Capacity could be increased with optional larger wing tanks (two at 50 US gal. each), or nacelle baggage locker transfer tanks (two at 26 US gal. each). The baggage locker tanks were initially introduced on the Cessna 411A, although the TCDS indicates that they are applicable to all models.

In service, the Cessna 411 was criticized as being somewhat expensive to operate, due in part to reduction gearbox reliability and engine overhaul lives, with the later 411A version being generally preferred.

N411PM is a Cessna
411A, at Terrill,
Texas. *Author*

Cessna 411A
VH-MWJ seen at
Goulburn, NSW,
Australia. *Jim Smith*

Cessna 401 and 402

The Cessna 401 and 402 were announced at the same time in November 1966. These types were developments of the Cessna 411 that were intended to be less expensive to buy and operate. Compared with the Cessna 411, the 401 and 402 used ungeared 300 hp Continental TSIO-520-E engines driving three blade propellers, located slightly farther out on the wing than on the 411. The vertical tail was also increased in chord and was of lower aspect ratio. Maximum take-off weight was 6,300 lb., 200 lb. less than that of the 411. Maximum landing weight was 6,200 lb.

The 401 and 402 were essentially identical, the Cessna 402 being intended for commercial use, with an easily reconfigured interior and strengthened cabin floor. Capacity was two crew and up to six passengers for the 401 and up to seven passengers for the 402 (eight for the 402A and B). The Cessna 402 was subsequently developed into the 402B and 402C Utililiner/Businessliner, with lengthened cabin and increased baggage capacity.

Both aircraft initially had four elliptical cabin windows, but from 1973, the 402B introduced a reconfigured cabin with five rectangular windows. In their initial form, the Cessna 401 and 402 were visually indistinguishable. An optional side hinged door alongside the airstair could be fitted to the Cessna 402.

The fuel was arranged in a number of tanks—twin tip tanks, wing tanks and optional nacelle baggage locker tanks. Standard fuel capacity was 102 US gallons, which could be increased to up to 184 US gallons if additional optional tanks were installed in the wings and the nacelle baggage lockers.

The Cessna 401 was produced in three models, the 401, 401A, and 401B, with only minor changes between these models. A single prototype (for both models) flew for the first time on August 21, 1965, and FAA type approval (for both types) was gained on September 20, 1966. Production of the Cessna 401 continued until May 1972, after which only the Cessna 402B and 402C were built.

The Cessna 402 was sold under four designations 402, 402A, 402B and 402C. The 402A (type approval January 1969) featured a 26 cu. ft. nose baggage compartment and other minor upgrades. The initial version of the 402B (approved November 1969) introduced a longer nose baggage compartment, compared to the 402A. Later 402B aircraft had lengthened cabins and revised glazing, as described below. The 402C had a revised fuel system (without tip tanks) and a number of other minor modifications.

From 1971 onward, the Cessna 402 was sold as either the Utililiner or Businessliner, dependent upon equipment fit and cabin layout. The initial Cessna 402B was configured for two crew and up to eight passengers. The overall length of this model was increased by 25 inches to 35ft 10in. The total baggage capacity for the early production 402B (up to c/n 402B1300) was 760 lb., distributed between nose, rear fuselage and engine nacelle baggage compartments.

G-AWXM is a Cessna 401, at Cranfield, Bedfordshire, UK. The Cessna 401 is similar to the Cessna 411 with a revised fin and rudder profile and ungeared engines. *Author*

SE-FXI is a Cessna 402B at Toussus-le-Noble in June 1981. The Cessna 402 is essentially identical to the Cessna 401, but optimized for quick change commercial and air taxi operations. *Author*

A 1967 Cessna 401 (c/n 401-0082 ex-N3282Q) G-AVKN rolls out after landing at Cranfield, Bedfordshire, UK. *Author*

Cessna 401 G-AVXN at Nottingham's Tollerton Airport,
prior to taking part in the 1970 King's Cup Air Race. *Author*

Cessna 402 VH-ELZ
in April 2004 at
Adelaide, SA,
Australia, showing
propeller damage
after a landing
accident. *Jim Smith*

From 1973 onward (c/n 402B1301 onward), the cabin in the Cessna 402B was increased in length by 16 inches and a new cabin window configuration, featuring five rectangular side windows, was introduced. Overall length was again increased slightly to 36ft 1in. Baggage capacity was significantly increased to no less than 1,340 lb.

The final model was the Cessna 402C, which featured a revised fuel system with a "wet wing." This model can be readily distinguished by its lack of wing tip fuel tanks. Engine power was increased by fitting two 325hp Continental TSIO-520-VB engines. This allowed the maximum weights to increase to 6,850 lb., for both take-off and landing.

Type approval for this model was gained on 25 September 1978 and the 402C remained in production until 1987. Wing span was significantly increased to 44ft 1½ in and length slightly increased to 36 ft. 4½in. Maximum baggage capacity for the 402C increased again to 1,500 lb. Fuel was carried in two integral wing tanks with a total usable capacity of 206 US gallons.

The total number of Cessna 401 and 402s produced was 2,190, with Airlife General Aviation indicating 545 Cessna 401 and 1,645 Cessna 402s, of which 1,526 are Cessna 402B and 402Cs.

D-ICFC is another Cessna 402B, at Blackbushe, Hampshire, UK. This is an example of the Utililiner variant. *Author*

G-GILL is an early Cessna 402C Businessliner II (c/n 402C0006) at Denham, Buckinghamshire, UK. *Author*

From 1973 onward, the Cessna 402B featured a stretched cabin with five rectangular side windows. VH-SVQ is a 1975 Cessna 402B, photographed in November 2008, at Archerfield, QLD, Australia, in the updated configuration. *Jim Smith*

The Cessna 402C is distinguished by its lack of tip tanks and greater wingspan. F-GFZZ is a 402C Businessliner III photographed at St. Brieuc, France, in 1989. *Jim Smith*

Cessna 421

The Cessna 421 was publicly announced at the end of October 1965, some two weeks after the prototype's first flight on October 14, 1965.

The 421 was essentially a pressurized derivative of the Cessna 411, using geared 375 hp Continental GTSIO-520-D engines and, like the Cessna 401 and 402, featuring an increase in fin chord compared with the Cessna 411.

A main distinguishing feature, which is common to other models with a pressurized fuselage, was a change to cockpit glazing. A triangular transparent panel was introduced at the base of the windscreen and the cockpit side window was reduced in size.

Four main models were produced, the C421, 421A, 421B and 421C. These are briefly discussed below, with a summary of their differences in specification and any other distinguishing features.

The Cessna 421 entered production having obtained type approval on May 1, 1967. The type was configured with six seats, for two crew and four passengers. The maximum take-off weight was 6,800 lb. (which could be increased to 6,840 lb. with appropriate flight manual revisions and implementation of an appropriate Cessna Service Kit).

The Cessna 421 is a pressurized and upgraded development of the Cessna 411. Belgian-registered Cessna 421A air taxi OO-LFC is seen here on short finals to land at Eastleigh Airport, Southampton, UK. *Author*

D-IAHS is a Cessna 421A (c/n 421A0050) at Blackbushe, Hampshire, UK. *Author*

N2249Q is a 1969 Cessna 421A (c/n 421A0049), at
Monterey, CA. *Author*

A total baggage load of 930 lb. could be accommodated
in nose, wing baggage locker, and fuselage compartments.
Fuel was carried in two wing tip tanks (usable capacity 50
US gallons each) and a pair of wing tanks each with 35 US
gallons usable capacity. Optionally, larger wing tanks and
wing locker transfer tanks could also be fitted for a maximum
fuel capacity of 248 US gallons.

The generally similar Cessna 421A received type approval
on November 19, 1968, and was cleared for a maximum
weight of 6,840 lb. from the outset.

Production of these two variants comprised 200 C421s,
and 158 C421As.

More significant changes were introduced with the
Cessna 421B Golden Eagle, which was announced in December
1969, and received its type approval on April 28, 1970. This
variant featured a lengthened nose with greater baggage
capacity; an increase in take-off weight to 7,250 lb.; and an
increase in wingspan to maintain performance at the higher
weight. Power was provided by two 375 hp Continental
GTSIO-520-H engines driving three bladed propellers.

A range of cabin configurations was available, allowing
the carriage of between four and eight passengers. An
additional side cabin window was introduced on this model.
After the first 200 aircraft, an increase of maximum take-
off weight to 7,450 lb. was approved. Maximum baggage

The Cessna 421B introduced a lengthened cabin and can be
distinguished by the combination of five elliptical windows
together with tip tanks. VH-ASE is a Cessna 421B
photographed at Essendon, VIC, Australia, in March 2009.
Jim Smith

capacity was 1,340 lb. (although this is reduced if the nose bay is also used for the installation of avionics). After the three-hundredth aircraft, this figure could be increased to 1,500 lb. The standard fuel capacity was 175 US gallons split between wing tip tanks and wing tanks. As with the C421, optional additional capacity could be provided by larger wing tanks and wing locker transfer tanks. Some 700 C421Bs were built.

The final version, the Cessna 421C, introduced similar changes to those described earlier for the Cessna 402C. These comprise a "wet wing" with no tip tanks of 41 ft. 1½ in span. The C421C entered production in 1976, having received type approval on October 28, 1975. Power was provided by two 375 hp GTSIO-520-L or –M1 engines.

Maximum take-off weight and baggage and cabin capacities remained unchanged. Standard fuel capacity (usable) was 206 US gallons. Optional wing locker transfer tanks can be fitted, increasing total fuel capacity to 262 US gallons. Dependent upon avionic fit, this model was sold as either the Golden Eagle II or Golden Eagle III, with additional equipment fitted as standard. Cessna 421C production is quoted as 859 examples.

A 1976 Cessna 421C G-RLMC on short finals to land at Blackbushe, Hampshire, UK. *Author*

The Cessna 421C adopted the "wet wing" as with the 402C, resulting in elimination of the wing tip-tanks and an increased span. N5363J is a 1980 Cessna 421C Golden Eagle III photographed for publicity purposes. *Cessna Aircraft Company*

Additional Cessna 421 Images

An understated color scheme emphasizes the clean lines of Cayman Islands-registered Cessna 421C VR-CPR, at Blackbushe, Hampshire, UK. *Author*

Cessna 421C G-OSAL at Blackbushe, Hampshire, UK. This aircraft was later modified to become the Meteorological Office Civil Contingencies Aircraft (MOCCA), which is discussed later under Cessna 400 specials. *Author*

Cessna 421C VH-NSW on the approach to Canberra Airport, ACT, Australia, in October 2008. *Jim Smith*

Cessna 414

The Cessna 414 is essentially a hybrid of a Cessna 402 wing with a Cessna 421 pressurized fuselage. The type was announced in December 1969, having flown for the first time on September 1, 1968, and received type approval on September 24, 1969.

The Cessna 414 was powered by two 310 hp ungeared Continental TSIO-520-J or –B engines driving three-bladed propellers. The engine installation is particularly clean and slim. Accommodation was normally provided for two crew and four or five passengers. Maximum allowable weights were 6,200 lb. for landing and 6,350 lb. for take-off. The type offers cruising speeds of around 200 kt at 25,000 ft.

Fuel was carried in twin tip tanks and wing tanks. Standard fuel capacity was 102 US gallons, which can be significantly increased to 203 US gallons if maximum optional tanks are installed in the wings and the nacelle baggage lockers. Baggage capacity was 930 lb. in nose, wing locker, and fuselage compartments, increasing in later production examples to 1,090 lb.

A new model, the C414A Chancellor, was introduced in 1978, featuring a "wet wing" with no tip tanks and being essentially a C402C wing married to a 421C fuselage having five cabin side windows.

The 414A received type approval on September 30, 1977, and was powered by two 310 hp Continental TSIO-520-NB engines. The wing span for this version was increased from 39 ft. 10¼ in to 44 ft. 1½ in.

The maximum take-off and landing weight of the 414A was increased to 6,750 lb. Alternative cabin layouts were available for two crew plus four to six passengers. As with the C421C, total baggage capacity is increased to 1,500 lb. with a lengthened nose. The standard usable fuel capacity

G-DYNE is a 1970 Cessna 414 (c/n 4140070) at Cranfield, Bedfordshire, UK. *Author*

was 206 US gallons. Quoted cruising speeds were 195 kt at 10,000 ft. and 225 kt at 24,500 ft.

The Chancellor II and Chancellor III sub-variants came with an increased level of standard equipment fit. The Cessna 414 and 414A remained in production until 1985, with total production figures of 516 C414 and 554 C414A being quoted (for example, by Wikipedia and in Airlife's General Aviation).

A number of after-market modifications are available to enhance the type's performance, including aerodynamic refinements, vortex generator kits, winglets, and engine enhancements. A series of such enhancements is offered, for example, by RAM Aircraft.

The Cessna 414 has the pressurized fuselage of the Cessna 421 married to the wing and ungeared engines of the Cessna 402. This is Irish-registered Cessna 414 EI-AWW on the approach to land at Biggin Hill, Kent, UK. *Author*

The Cessna 414A Chancellor was an upgraded Cessna 414 with the same modifications as had been introduced on the Cessna 402C and 421C, providing a "wet wing" of increased span and elimination of the tip tanks. N5252J is the subject of a very nice air to air publicity photograph. *Cessna Aircraft Company*

A fine Cessna photograph of Chancellor II N2618Y. *Cessna Aircraft Company*

N2742A is a RAM-modified Cessna 414A Chancellor, this is a RAM series IV aircraft with vortex generator kit on wings and fin and aerodynamic turning vanes on the engine nacelles. *Author*

Cessna 404 Titan

The Cessna 404 built upon the success of the Cessna 402C with increased power and passenger accommodation. The main external distinguishing features are the dihedral tailplane, geared piston engines, and stretched cabin with six side windows. The aircraft is typically configured with ten or eleven seats (including those for the crew).

The prototype N5404J flew for the first time on February 26, 1975, receiving its FAA type approval on July 21, 1976. Power was provided by two 375 hp Continental GTSIO-520-M geared supercharged piston engines driving three-bladed propellers.

Maximum take-off weight is 8,400 lb., but landing weight is restricted to 8,100 lb. Nevertheless, these figures represent a significant increase in disposable load compared to the Cessna 402C, with its take-off and landing weight of 6,850 lb.

As with the Cessna 402C and 421C, maximum baggage load is 1,500 lb. split between nose, wing locker, and fuselage compartments. The standard usable fuel capacity is 340 US gallons.

A total of 396 Cessna 404s were built, the type being widely used for passenger (Titan Ambassador), utility (Titan Courier), and cargo operations (Titan Freighter).

A classic Cessna publicity photograph of the first Cessna 404 Titan N3928C (c/n 4040001) taken in 1977. *Cessna Aircraft Company*

The Cessna 404 is essentially a stretched Cessna 402C with geared engines, dihedral tailplane, and additional cabin glazing. This side on air-to-air photograph emphasizes the length of the aircraft. N8854G is a 1977 Titan Courier (c/n 4040094). *Cessna Aircraft Company*

This Guinea-registered Cessna 404 Titan II 3X-GCF was photographed at Cranfield, Bedfordshire, UK in July 1992. *Author*

VH-VEA seen with Corporate Air at Goulburn, NSW, Australia, in April 2013. *Author*

1981 Cessna 404 VH-ENT at Adelaide in October 2006. *Author*

Titan II VH-VEA on the sunny apron at its normal home base of Canberra Airport, ACT, Australia, in 2005. *Jim Smith*

Flying the Cessna 404

The following contribution from Patrick Caruth is gratefully acknowledged. In 1981, he travelled to Aberdeen with a brand-new Commercial Pilot License to work for an air taxi company called Perigrine Air Services. He writes:

"Being young and inexperienced, I started doing night mail and freight on the Piper Aztec, while keenly eyeing up the three beautiful Cessna Titans on the fleet.

"A year later, I was allowed onto them. Sitting in the front, the first thing that you notice is the long, elegant nose stretching ahead of you. Then there are those engines, huge 375 hp Teledyne Continentals, also stretching way out in front, all giving the impression of flying some kind of Starship.

"The flight deck is also wide with complete dual controls and instruments. All the avionics were of the traditional Cessna series and the type also had an effective autopilot.

"Fuel control was simple—on and off each side, with a cross-feed. And HUGE tanks; one could fly for nine hours with four passengers and there are reports of flights up to eleven hours. Legs from Aberdeen to Barcelona were often done. With eleven passengers, or a ton of freight, you could just do our standard 'milk run' from Aberdeen to Stavanger in Norway.

"In terms of field performance, you didn't really want to accept runways of less than 1,000m (3,280 ft). I think that Scatsa in the Shetland Islands was the shortest regular destination at 960m (3,150 ft).

"Flying the aircraft was a delight, with well-harmonized controls. On one engine, it would struggle at maximum weight and had to be flown accurately. Careful engine management was the key to preserving their life. They simply did not like being mishandled, either in terms of shock cooling in the descent, or aggressive throttle movements.

Our standard procedure was as follows:

"Full throttle for take-off; set climb power to cruise altitude; set cruise power and leave the throttles in the descent, just changing attitude to achieve a descent rate of 500 ft/min (unpressurized aircraft); try not to touch the throttles until shortish finals.

"The first stage flap and gear limiting speeds were very high (182 kt), allowing them to be deployed early. This was very helpful when, for example, going into Gatwick, where you had to maintain 160 kt until four miles out.

Aberdeen-based 1978 Cessna 404 Titan G-BKTW of Peregrine Air Services. *Patrick Caruth*

The clean instrument panel and controls of the 1979 Cessna 404 Titan Courier. *Cessna Aircraft Company*

Titan G-BKWA (c/n 4040061) takes off from Cranfield, Bedfordshire, UK. *Author*

A 1977 Cessna 404 Titan G-BKWA climbs away. *Author*

N4489L (c/n 4040029) outside Cessna Distributor Rogers Aviation's hangar at Cranfield Airport, Bedfordshire UK. This aircraft is now registered HC-BTM in Ecuador. *Author*

"On landing, the excellent trailing link undercarriage always enhanced the touchdown. Crosswinds were no problem, just crab it in, kick off the drift, and she would sit down like a baby.

"Icing was more of a problem as it collected on the wings fairly quickly, certainly more rapidly than was the case with the Aztec. One would generally let no more than an inch build up and then deploy the rubber boots to crack off the ice (allegedly). The propeller de-ice would fire bits of ice into the side of the fuselage like a machine gun. This would scare the pilot … and terrify the passengers!

"We also used to operate the Fishery Protection flights around the Scottish coasts and islands … from Shetland down to Prestwick on the west coast. With engine management in mind, we used to fly at around 500 ft. at a low cruise setting and then deploy one stage of flap to maneuver around a fishing boat at around 500 ft. One could then fly a five hour sortie hardly ever needing to move the throttles.

"The fishermen could always hear us coming, so there was a certain amount of cunning and 'cat and mouse' tactics involved. On one occasion, we ran alongside a boat to take its photo and all the crew were on its side. They promptly dropped their trousers and 'mooned' at us. The Agriculture and Fisheries Department were not amused, as we failed to delete the image from their file.

"Another regular trip was what we used to call the 'Bomb Run' for the Atomic Energy Establishment. About once a month, we would fly to Dounreay and pick up two large lead-lined containers of spent Uranium 235 and fly them down to RAF Abingdon, from which they would go off to Harwell.

"The containers only just fitted in (with all the seats out). They were accompanied by an armed policeman, who sat in the very rear seat, with the (obligatory) two pilots up front. His job during the flight was to make tea and coffee. Unfortunately, it was impossible to get from the back to the front because of the size of the containers. The trick was slide the cups as far as possible along the top of the containers and them help them forward by gently pushing the nose down. Needless to say, there were a lot of coffee stains!

"On another occasion, I took eleven farmers from Inverness to Coventry for a day at the Royal Agricultural Show. This was only just possible within fuel, weight, and balance limits. When they came back, they were all clutching their 'freebie' handouts, which included a sack of potatoes for each of them. We used up every inch of Coventry's runway that hot afternoon.

"As I remember, we worked on 120 kt for the climb and 180 kt TAS for the cruise (making navigation calculations relatively easy). Cruise power settings were, I believe, a relatively low rpm (around 1,900) and up to 24 lb./square inch manifold pressure.

"I never had any major problems with the aircraft or its engines, as we looked after them and had excellent engineers. Other operators did have problems, usually due to mismanaging the engines. All in all, very happy memories of a lovely aeroplane, on which I have around 500 hours flown between 1982 and 1986, alongside the Aztec and Beech Super King Air—another lovely airplane."

Cessna 441

The Cessna 441 Conquest pressurized turboprop executive and third level feeder liner was announced in November 1974, the prototype N441CC flying for the first time on August 28, 1975. FAA type approval was gained on August 19, 1977. The aircraft normally accommodates a single pilot and eight to ten passengers, although alternative seating arrangements are also available.

The Conquest is essentially a development of the Cessna 404, with the chief distinguishing features being the slim nacelles of the Garrett turboprop engines and the six cabin side windows, which are rectangular with generous well-rounded corners. Compared with the Titan, the wingspan is increased by three feet to 46 ft. 4 in.

The prototype Cessna 441 Conquest N441CC during its test flight program. The Cessna 441 is a pressurized, turboprop-powered development of the Cessna Titan, used for commuter and third-level airline service. *Cessna Aircraft Company*

Cessna 441 N8881N photographed at McCarran International Airport, Las Vegas, Nevada, in February 1981. *Author*

**A Cessna publicity photograph of Cessna Conquest
N9123G.** *Cessna Aircraft Company*

A 1983 Cessna 441 VH-VED on final approach against the backdrop of the sunny skies of Canberra, ACT, Australia. *Jim Smith*

Power is provided by two Garrett TPE331-8 engines driving three-blade propellers. These engines are flat-rated to 635.5 shp each up to 16,000 ft. Some aircraft are fitted with smaller diameter four blade propellers, offering improved performance and reduced cabin noise levels. Aftermarket modification can include the fitting of Garrett TPE331-10 engines. Maximum all up weight limits are 9,850 lb. for take-off and 9,360 lb. for landing. Maximum baggage capacity is 1,500 lb., split between a nose compartment and baggage space to the rear of the cabin. The usable fuel capacity is 475 US gallons in two integral wing tanks.

Indicative performance includes a cruising speed of up to 290 kt at 24,000 ft. Maximum operating speed is 245 kt up to 21,300 ft. and a maximum Mach number of 0.55 above that altitude.

Range figures depend on the number of passengers carried and the cruise altitude used. With eleven persons on board, figures between 1,000 nm and 1,300 nm can be achieved, the latter figure requiring a cruise altitude of 33,000 ft. The maximum operating altitude was initially 33,000 ft., this being increased to 35,000 ft. from c/n 441-0173 onward.

After the Cessna 425 Corsair was renamed the Conquest I (see below), the Cessna 441 was marketed as the Conquest II. In total, 362 Cessna 441s were built.

Rossair Cessna 441 VH-XMD (c.n 4410025) at its Adelaide Airport home base on October 31, 2006. *Author*

Cessna 441 VH-VEM at its home base of Canberra Airport, ACT, Australia. *Jim Smith*

A 1978 Cessna 441 VH-OCS (c/n 4410030) approaching to land at Adelaide, SA, Australia, in 2007. *Jim Smith*

O'Connor Airlines Conquest II VH-OAA photographed at Adelaide Airport on October 31, 2006. *Author*

Cessna 425 Corsair and Conquest I

The Cessna 425 was, in effect a turboprop derivative of the Cessna 421C, aimed to provide a lower cost and higher performance competitor to the Beech King Air. The first prototype flew for the first time on September 12, 1978, FAA type approval being gained on July 1, 1980.

Power was provided by two Pratt & Whitney PT6A-112 engines, flat rated to 450 shp. The aircraft is normally configured for one or two crew plus four cabin passengers, but alternative seating arrangements allow up to six cabin passengers to be carried. The maximum take-off weight was initially 8,200 lb. (Corsair), this being increased to 8,600 lb. from c/n 177 onward (Conquest I). Earlier aircraft could be modified with a Cessna service kit to operate at the higher weight, then being renamed as Conquest I to reflect this change.

G-BJET is an early production Corsair (c/n 4250024) at Cranfield, Bedfordshire, UK. This aircraft was subsequently sold in Finland. *Author*

The Cessna 425 is, in essence, a turboprop Cessna 421C powered by two PT6A engines. G-ONOR is a 1983 Corsair at Blackbushe, Hampshire, UK. *Author*

The Cessna 425 Corsair was developed to provide Cessna with an entry-level turboprop to compete with aircraft like the Beech King Air. The type was later renamed the Conquest I. This dramatic photograph of the first Corsair N2907A (c/n 4250001) dates from 1981. *Cessna Aircraft Company*

N6772B is a Cessna Corsair (c/n 4250020) being displayed at the Paris Air Show, Le Bourget, France. *Author*

The total baggage capacity is 1,100 lb. and the usable fuel capacity is 366 US gallons. The maximum operating altitude is 30,000 ft., at which height cruising speeds of 210 kt to 250 kt are available, dependent on power setting and range requirements. Maximum range is in excess of 1,100 nm. Maximum operating speed below 21,800 ft. is 230 kt; above this altitude, the limit is expressed as a maximum operating Mach number of 0.52.

A total of 236 Cessna 425s were built, made up of 176 Corsairs and 70 Conquest Is, although many Corsair aircraft will have been subsequently modified to the later standard. Production was halted in 1986.

The aircraft is subject to periodic mandatory inspections of the tailplane, elevators, and elevator tabs to maintain their structural integrity.

Reims Cessna F406 Caravan II

The final variant of the Cessna 400 series, and the longest enduring in production terms, was the Reims-built Cessna F406 Caravan II. This aircraft is a turboprop derivative of the Cessna 404 Titan and has carved out a niche for itself as a long-endurance special operations aircraft, in addition to its primary role as a passenger and freight transport.

The French company Reims Aviation, part-owned by Cessna, produced Cessna products under license from 1960 onward. French-built aircraft are distinguished by an F at the start of their designation and ranged from the F150F through to the F337H Super Skymaster.

The Reims F406 Caravan II prototype F-WZLT was first shown, prior to its first flight, at the 1983 Paris Air Show. The first flight was made on September 22, 1983. French certification was achieved on December 21, 1984, with FAA type approval following on June 27, 1986. The first production aircraft flew on April 20, 1985, and an initial production run of eighty-five aircraft was planned.

The F406 has carved out a niche as a special operations aircraft, particularly for border protection and maritime and fisheries patrol work. This example, F-ZBFA, is being displayed at the Paris Air Show, Le Bourget, France, with an under-fuselage sideways-looking airborne radar (SLAR) pod. *Author*

A Cessna photograph of the US demonstrator of the Reims Cessna F406 Caravan II. Although this aircraft carries the serial F406 0001 on its fin, it was not in fact the first of the type to fly, that being F-WZLT. *Cessna Aircraft Company*

A 2008 F406 G-TDSA taking off from Farnborough, Hampshire, UK, in April 2012. This aircraft also has an under-fuselage equipment bay, possibly for aerial survey work. *Author*

A 1991 F406 G-CVXN "Caledonian Vixen" on final approach at the 2012 Farnborough Air Show, in July 2012. This aircraft has a maritime surveillance radar under the fuselage; there is also a mounting plate ahead of the nosewheel, possibly for an IR sensor turret. *Author*

The F406 is, in effect, a modified Cessna 404 Titan fitted with two 500hp Pratt & Whitney PT6A-112 turboprop engines. The FAA type approval lists a maximum take-off and landing weight of 9,360 lb., although the GECI Aviation website indicates that this figure has been increased to 9,850 lb., with plans for a further increase to 10,500 lb.

The maximum operating speed (FAA) between sea level and 21,500 ft. is 229 kt, changing to a maximum operating Mach number of 0.52 above that altitude. Maximum operating altitude is 30,000 ft. Seats are proved for a maximum of two crew and twelve passengers, although one or two crew and up to nine passengers is more typical.

Baggage is carried in nose and fuselage compartments and engine nacelle lockers. Additional capacity can be provided with an optional under-fuselage baggage pod. Maximum usable fuel load is 475 US gallons. The GECI Aviation website indicates that engine nacelle tanks will shortly be available, increasing the fuel capacity by a further 50 US gallons.

The manufacturer's performance data includes a maximum cruise speed of 246 kt at 15,000 ft., a more typical cruise speed being around 200 kt. The cruising speed for maximum range is 186 kt at 10,000 ft., allowing a range of 1,290 nm to be achieved with forty-five minutes

Demonstration F406 F-GKRA on display at the Farnborough Air Show in 1990. *Author*

reserves. High endurance patrol operations are possible, with up to six hours endurance available, also with forty-five minutes reserves.

In addition to passenger and cargo transport roles, the F406 has been successfully deployed in many special mission configurations. Equipment fit in these roles includes radar and infra-red sensors, aerial survey equipment and, for the French Armée de l'Air, target towing equipment. Special mission roles include maritime surveillance (including border security, customs, and fishery patrols); pollution control; aerial photography and survey; target towing.

Operators include the French Gendarmerie and Customs services, Australian Customs, and the Greek coast guard. Aircraft are also operated in support of fisheries protection in the UK and Namibia.

The GECI Aviation website indicated (in 2013) that a fleet of eighty-three aircraft was being supported at that time. The company has since entered liquidation.

F406 G-BVJT climbs out at Farnborough, Hampshire, UK, in April 2012. This is another example with an under-fuselage equipment bay. *Author*

Caravan II "Caledonian Vixen" belonging to Caledonian Airborne Systems just before touchdown. Lettering on the fuselage indicates that a long range Selex Seaspray 7300 Scorpio active electronically scanned array (AESA) radar is fitted. *Author*

Recognizing the Cessna 400 Series

The main features that can be used to identify different models within the Cessna 400 series are as follows: shape of tail fin; engine installation (geared or ungeared piston engines, or turboprops); tailplane dihedral; and number and shape of windows. The presence or absence of wing tip tanks also distinguishes some specific models.

The photographs below provide a series of comparisons to assist identification, together with some explanatory text to highlight differences.

First: geared or ungeared piston engines.
The image on the left shows a geared engine installation on a Cessna 404 Titan. Because of the propeller gear mechanism, the propeller is raised above the air intakes, with a humped fairing running along the top of the engine cowling. On the right is a Cessna 401 with a very clean and shallow engine installation.

Next: fin and rudder proportions.
This is of particular significance to distinguishing the Cessna 411 from later models such as the Cessna 401, 402, 414, and 421.

The aircraft at bottom left is a Cessna 411. The portion of the fixed fin ahead of the rudder aerodynamic balance is noticeably narrower than the same area on the Cessna 402, shown at bottom right.

Pressurized or unpressurized fuselage. The Cessna 414, 421, 425, and 441 all have pressurized fuselages. This can be seen in the cockpit glazing, where the pressurized aircraft have a small triangular side window at the base of the main windscreen on both sides of the fuselage.

At top right on this page is an unpressurized Cessna 401, whose cockpit glazing can be directly compared with the pressurized Cessna 414, second down on right.

Geared engine installation (on Cessna 404). *Author*

Ungeared engine installation (on Cessna 401). *Author*

Cessna 411 narrow chord fin. *Author*

Broader chord fin (on Cessna 402, but applies to many other models). *Author*

The combination of a pressurized fuselage and geared engines distinguishes the Cessna 421 from the Cessna 414 (see photograph at bottom left on P.121).

The next models between which there is some scope for confusion are the Cessna 402C and the Cessna 404 Titan. Both of these aircraft feature unpressurized aircraft with rectangular windows and no tip tanks. In the case of the 402C, there are five cabin side windows, whereas there are six on the Cessna 404. Another immediately distinguishing feature between these types is that the Cessna 402 (photo below) does not have tailplane dihedral, whereas the Cessna 404 (on the right) does. Furthermore, the Titan has geared engines, whereas the Cessna 402C does not.

In the case of the series production turbo prop aircraft, the main distinguishing features are the turboprop engine installation and the cockpit and cabin windows.

Cockpit glazing with unpressurized fuselage (on Cessna 401). *Author*

Cockpit glazing with triangular "quarterlight" on pressurized fuselage (on Cessna 414). *Author*

Five rectangular windows and no tailplane dihedral on a Cessna 402B. *Author*

Six rectangular windows and a dihedral tailplane on a Cessna 404 Titan. *Author*

The F406 has six rectangular windows and is unpressurized. Its dihedral tailplane is mounted partway up the tail fin.

The Cessna 441 Conquest II is pressurized and has rounded corners to its otherwise rectangular windows.

The Cessna 425 is pressurized and has five elliptical cabin windows. It also has engine nacelles that protrude beyond the wing trailing edge.

A model by model summary of the differences between the various models based on these features is given below:

Cessna 411: geared piston engines, unpressurized, four elliptical cabin windows, narrow chord fin.
Cessna 401 and 402 and 402A: ungeared engines, unpressurized, increased fin chord, no tailplane dihedral. Cessna 402B as above with five rectangular cabin windows; C402C as C402B with increased span and no tip tanks.
Cessna 421: geared engines, pressurized fuselage, four elliptical cabin windows, broader chord fin, tip tanks. Cessna 421B, as above with five elliptical cabin windows. C421C as C421B with increased span and no tip tanks.
Cessna 414: ungeared engines, pressurized fuselage, four elliptical cabin windows, C414A Chancellor as C414 with five elliptical cabin windows, increased span and no tip tanks.
Cessna 404: geared engines, six rectangular cabin windows, dihedral tailplane, no tip tanks.
Cessna 441: turboprop engines, pressurized, six rectangular cabin windows with rounded corners, no tip tanks.
Cessna 425: turboprop engines, pressurized fuselage, no tip tanks, five elliptical cabin windows.
Reims Cessna F406: turboprop engines, unpressurized fuselage, six rectangular cabin windows, no tip tanks, dihedral tailplane mounted partway up the fin.

Pressurized fuselage, windows with rounded corners and turboprop engines on the Cessna 441 Conquest II. *Author*

PT6 engines, dihedral tailplane partway up the fin, and six rectangular windows mean that this is a Reims Cessna F406 Caravan II.

The combination of pressurized fuselage and geared engines reveals this as a Cessna 421. *Cessna Aircraft Company*

A Cessna 425 Conquest I G-BNDY at Blackpool in 2001. Key features are the PT6 engines, extended nacelles, pressurized fuselage, and five elliptical windows. *Jim Smith*

Cessna 400 specials (RAM, STOL, MOCCA), and Turbine Conversions

RAM and STOL Modifications

As with the Cessna 300 series, there are a range of after-market modifications for the Cessna 400 series to improve both cruise and take-off and landing performance. Examples of such modifications include a range of variants from RAM Aircraft of Waco, Texas, and STOL modifications from Sierra Industries of Uvalde, Texas.

James L. Robertson pioneered the development of short take-off and landing (STOL) modifications for single and twin engine American general aviation aircraft from Beechcraft, Cessna, and Piper. These kits were sold through the Robertson Aircraft Corporation. In 1985, R/STOL Systems Inc. of Raleigh, Durham, North Carolina, took over the Robertson assets and continued marketing STOL packages for a very wide range of aircraft. This was taken over by Sierra Industries in September 1986.

RAM offers enhancements for piston engine models in the Cessna 400 series, including the C401, C402 through to C402C, 414 and 414A, and 421C. These modifications typically include increased installed power, aerodynamic refinements including winglets (in which case a "W" is appended to the model designation), cleaned-up engine nacelles. In some models, an increase in maximum weight is also offered. Clearance for flight into known icing is also offered in some cases.

Despite the significant range of modifications, there is often little to distinguish RAM-modified aircraft from the normal production aircraft, other than, perhaps, a discreet logo on the fuselage side or engine cowling, or winglets at the wingtips, where applicable.

Sierra Industries offers STOL modifications for all models in the C401, C402, C414, and C421 range. These aircraft normally feature the large Fowler flaps, leading edge cuffs, airflow vanes on the engine nacelles and the wing root, and wing vortex generators. The 1990–91 edition of *Janes All the World's Aircraft* indicates that the Cessna 400 package includes full span Fowler flaps and flap-linked drooping ailerons, a double hinged rudder and a longitudinal trim system that is automatically adjusted when the flaps are lowered.

The photograph (below left) depicts a winglet-equipped RAM Series VII Cessna 414AW, which is also fitted with STOL modifications, including Fowler flaps, vortex generators, and engine nacelle airflow vanes.

An upgraded Cessna 414A Chancellor, in this case a RAM Series VII model.
Jerry Temple Aviation

Robertson STOL Cessna 421C G-ISAR flying over Henstridge, Somerset in March 2016. The large area-increasing flaps associated with the STOL modification are very evident.

MOCCA (Meteorological Office Civil Contingency Aircraft)

In 2010, the Eyjafjallajökull volcano erupted, producing a large cloud of fine ash particles that was spread by the prevailing winds over much of Western Europe. Because ingestion of these particles can produce damaging depositions in gas turbine engines, much of European and North Atlantic airspace was closed to air travel for more than a week, producing significant and widespread disruption to passenger air travel.

During this event, there was significant debate around the accuracy of modeling of the ash dispersal field. Partly because of this, the UK Civil Aviation Authority has procured a modified Cessna 421C, capable of collecting significant data from within ash clouds and also responding to other significant civil contingency events. This is known as MOCCA—the Meteorological Office Civil Contingency Aircraft.

The choice of the Cessna 421 was based on the fact that it is a reliable pressurized airframe with sufficient cabin volume for equipment integration. Its flight envelope allows operation at altitudes that are relevant to both commercial aviation and volcanic ash dispersal.

The instruments and equipment fitted are suitable not only for ash monitoring, but also for measuring other gas and pollutant concentrations.

The equipment fit is illustrated below (reproduced courtesy of the UK Meteorological Office).

The various instruments measure temperature, pressure, humidity (AIMMS probe on port wing tip); cloud aerosol

G-HIJK is the Meteorological Office Civil Contingencies Aircraft and is fitted with extensive equipment to monitor airborne gases and particles, including volcanic ash. It is seen here on the approach to Bournemouth Airport, Hurn, UK, in September 2012. *Jim Smith*

particle and micrometeor size (CAPS probe mounted on the port wingtip); and a LIDAR (UV laser sensor) to measure particle distribution above and below the aircraft by backscattered light.

The fuselage-mounted LIDAR can be mounted pre-flight to be directed upward or downward, dependent on the experimental plan. An air intake allows air samples to be routed to other instruments to collect further gaseous data including sulphur dioxide concentrations.

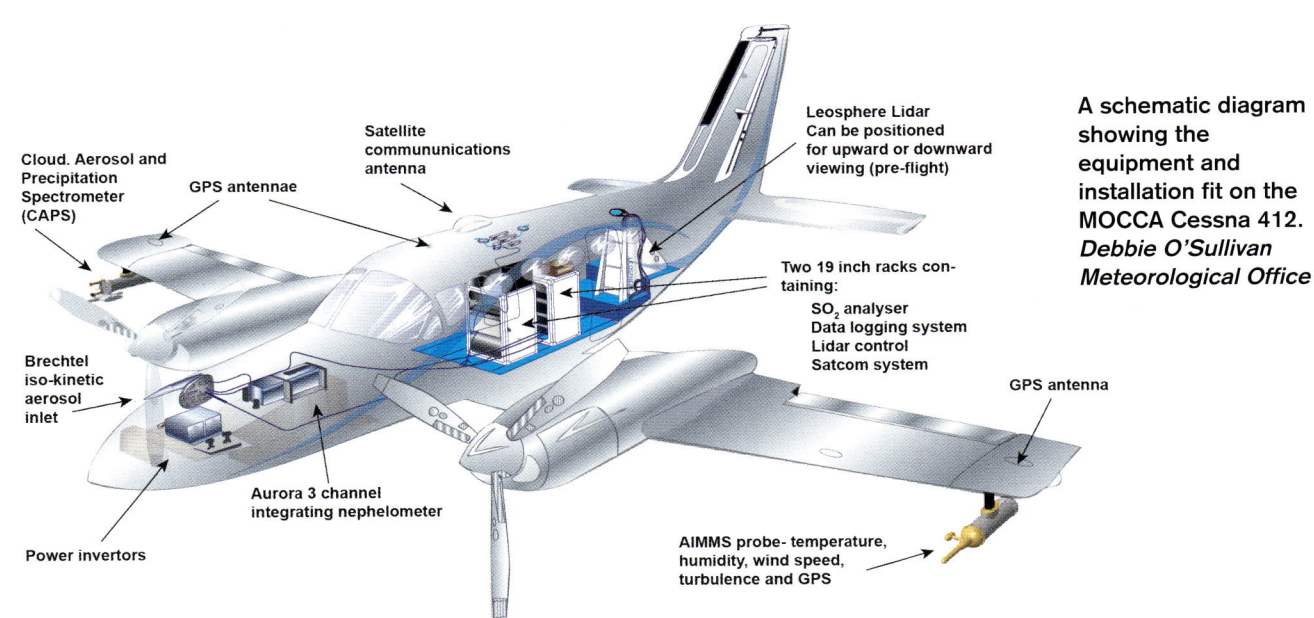

Cloud. Aerosol and Precipitation Spectrometer (CAPS)

GPS antennae

Satellite commununications antenna

Leosphere Lidar Can be positioned for upward or downward viewing (pre-flight)

Two 19 inch racks containing:

SO$_2$ analyser
Data logging system
Lidar control
Satcom system

GPS antenna

Brechtel iso-kinetic aerosol inlet

Aurora 3 channel integrating nephelometer

Power invertors

AIMMS probe- temperature, humidity, wind speed, turbulence and GPS

A schematic diagram showing the equipment and installation fit on the MOCCA Cessna 412. *Debbie O'Sullivan Meteorological Office*

Cessna 400 Series Modifications to Turboprop Power

Turboprop adaptations of Cessna 402 and 414 were developed by American Jet Industries, who sold the design rights to these models to Scenic Airways of Las Vegas, Nevada. These models are known as the Turbo Star 402 and Turbo Star Pressurized 414. First flight of the Turbo Star 402 was made on June 10, 1970.

Replacement of the piston engines allows both a saving in empty weight and an increase in maximum weight. Fuel capacity was increased from 126 US gallons to 200 US gallons. The Turbo Star 402 is powered by two 400 shp Allison 250-B17 turboprops.

A review of entries in *Janes All the World's Aircraft* reveals a significant number of adaptations of further Cessna 400 series models, including the following:

The Riley Turbine Rocket 421 with two flat-rated LTP 101-700 engines. First flight of the prototype was made on January 10, 1978, with the initial production aircraft following on 4 June. This model offered a maximum take-off weight of 7,650 lb. A subsequent model, the Riley Turbine Eagle 421 was a Cessna 421C powered by two Pratt & Whitney PT6A-135 and was subsequently marketed as the Advanced Aircraft Regent 1500, with maximum take-off weight of 7,600 lb. and maximum landing weight of 7,200 lb.

Two Cessna 404 Titan turbine conversions are listed, the Riley Turbine 404 and the Omni Titan Turbo Titan from a company based in Rockville, Maryland. This model was powered by two 650 hp Pratt & Whitney PT6A-34 and was cleared for maximum weights of 8450 lb. for take-off and 8,100 lb. for landing.

One other Riley model listed is the Cessna 414A-derived Riley Turbine Chancellor.

The final photograph shows N1MF, an unidentified turbine conversion of a Cessna 421B, at Cranfield, Bedfordshire in July 1986. This model is not PT6A-powered—the PT6A is a reverse-flow engine with its exhausts at the front of the engine nacelles. The engine installation shows a large exhaust tailpipe to the rear of the nacelle and the FAA registration database simply lists the engine type as "Experimental."

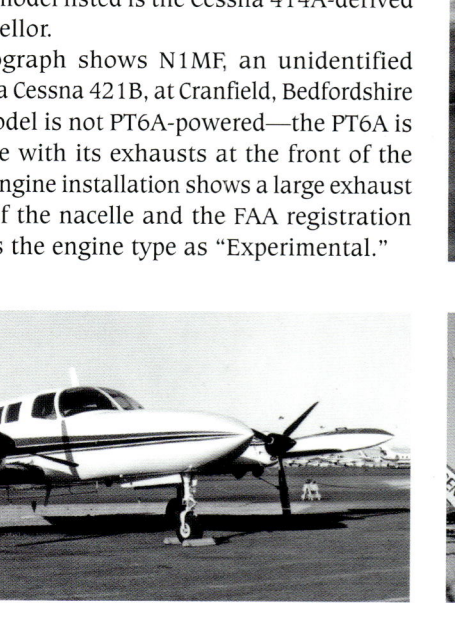

Scenic Aviation Turbo Star 402 N50SA at McCarran International Airport, Las Vegas, Nevada, in February 1981. *Author*

N525SA is a turboprop Cessna 414 conversion known as the Turbo Star Pressurized 414. *Author*

Turbo Star 402 N50SA parked in front of Scenic Aviation's "Home of the Tin Goose" in Las Vegas, Nevada. *Author*

N1MF is an experimental turboprop conversion of a Cessna 412B at Cranfield, Bedfordshire, UK, in July 1986. *Author*

Fighter-like Cessna 301C VH-DBA, at Avalon, VIC, Australia. *Jim Smith*

The Cessna 300 and 400 Series Family

With the introduction of the fighter-like Cessna 310 from 1953, Cessna effectively redefined high performance twin engine aircraft for personal and business use. This long-lived and successful design remained in production until 1981, with some 5,737 being built, together with 577 of the closely related Cessna 320.

In the mid-1960s, Cessna developed a family of cabin-class twin-engine aircraft known as the Cessna 400 series, beginning initially with the Cessna 411. This stimulated the parallel development of three new cabin-class twins in the 300-series, these being the Cessna T303, 335, and 340.

Ultimately, the total number of conventionally configured Cessna 300-series twin engine aircraft built reached nearly 8,000.

With all up weights ranging from the initial Cessna 310 figure of 4,600 lb. through 6,290 lb. for a pressurized Cessna 340A fitted with a vortex generator kit, the range offers high performance across the board, combined with comfort and practicality.

The Cessna 400 series runs from the 6,500 lb. Cessna 411 business and executive aircraft, through to the Cessna 9,850 lb. 441 Conquest II third level airliner. With both pressurized and non-pressurized models and a wide range of cabin accommodation, the family provides platforms for private ownership, business, air taxi, feeder-liner, and special mission uses. This philosophy served Cessna well, with some 6,500 aircraft in the Cessna 400 series being delivered.

With some 14,500 aircraft in the combined family of popular Cessna twins, produced from 1953 to 1987 (and beyond, in the case of the F406), the importance of these high performance and versatile aircraft is more than evident.

The final and most sophisticated of the Cessna twins is the Cessna 441 Conquest II. This example, VH-OAA, was photographed at Adelaide, SA, Australia, in 2006. *Jim Smith*

Classic Light Aircraft: An Illustrated Look, 1920s to the Present. Ron Smith. A richly illustrated A to Z book exploring the huge variety of light aircraft to be found at smaller airfields around the world. Mass production types, homebuilts and rare survivors of older aircraft are included, together with description of the types and indications of how many were built. Size: 7" x 10" • 849 color and b/w images • 416 pp ISBN: 978-0-7643-4896-9 • hard cover • $34.99